SHAPING THE
LEARNING CURVE

SHAPING THE LEARNING CURVE

Essays on Economic Education

Edited by Franklin G. Mixon, Jr.

iUniverse, Inc.
New York Lincoln Shanghai

Shaping the Learning Curve
Essays on Economic Education

Copyright © 2005 by Franklin G. Mixon, Jr.

iUniverse books may be ordered through booksellers or by contacting:

iUniverse
2021 Pine Lake Road, Suite 100
Lincoln, NE 68512
www.iuniverse.com
1-800-Authors (1-800-288-4677)

ISBN-13: 978-0-595-33806-1 (pbk)
ISBN-13: 978-0-595-78595-7 (ebk)
ISBN-10: 0-595-33806-2 (pbk)
ISBN-10: 0-595-78595-6 (ebk)

Printed in the United States of America

Contents

Part III. The Sociology of Economic Education

Contributors

Franklin G. Mixon, Jr. is the Business Advisory Council Professor of Economics at The University of Southern Mississippi. Professor Mixon was the recipient of the Business Advisory Council Outstanding Faculty Award (2001). He currently serves on the editorial board of the *Journal of Economics and Finance Education*. He has contributed economic education scholarship to the *Journal of Economic Education*, the *Journal of Economics and Finance Education*, and the *Journal of Education for Business*. Professor Mixon's research outside the field of economic education focuses mainly on public choice, and has been published in the *Journal of Money, Credit, and Banking*, the *Southern Economic Journal* and *Public Choice*.

H. Tyrone Black is Professor of Economics at The University of Southern Mississippi. Professor Black is the coauthor (with Donnie Daniel) of the text *Money and Banking: Contemporary Practices, Policies, and Issues* (3rd edition, McGraw-Hill, 1988), and his work on student achievement in business programs has appeared in the *Journal of Education for Business*. Outside of the area of business and economic education, Professor Black's research on legislatures and other topics has been published in *Public Choice, Industrial Relations* and *Social Science Quarterly*.

Steven B. Caudill is the Regions Bank Professor of Economics at Auburn University. Professor Caudill was awarded the Panhellenic Council Outstanding Professor Award (1997, 1998, 2000 and 2003), the AGBS Teacher of the Year Award (1999 and 2003), and the Economics Department Outstanding Teacher Award (2000). He currently serves on the editorial board of the *Journal of Economics and Finance Education* and he has contributed economic education scholarship to the *Journal of Economic Education*. Professor Caudill's work in applied econometrics has been published in the *Journal of Econometrics, Review of Economics and Statistics*, and the *Journal of Business and Economic Statistics*.

Trellis G. Green is Associate Professor of Economics at The University of Southern Mississippi. He has contributed economic education research to the

Journal of Economics and Finance Education. His work outside the field of economic education has been primarily in the area of environment and resource economics, and has been published in *Land Economics, Ecological Economics,* and *Society and Natural Resources.*

Paul W. Grimes is Professor of Economics and Chair of the Department of Finance and Economics and Director of the Center for Economic Education and Financial Literacy at Mississippi State University. Professor Grimes served (1991) as a Senior Evaluation Scholar in the Choices and Changes Program of the National Council on Economic Education. Before that, he served as a Pew Trust Summer Visiting Fellow at Princeton University (1988), where he assisted with the Research Workshop on Economic Education. Professor Grimes is the recipient of two Outstanding Faculty Member Awards (1998 and 2000) from the College of Business and Industry at MSU, and one President's Special Teaching Projects Award (1987). His research on economic education has appeared in the *Journal of Economic Education, Journal of Education for Business, Journal of Economics and Economic Education Research, College Student Journal, Computers and Education, The American Journal of Distance Education,* and *Collegiate Microcomputer.* He is also a coauthor of the text *Economics of Social Issues* (16th Edition, Irwin/McGraw-Hill, 2004). His research outside of the field of economic education has appeared in the *Journal of Urban Economics, Industrial Relations,* and the *Journal of Labor Research.*

Daniel M. Gropper is Associate Professor of Economics and Assistant Dean and Executive Director of the MBA Programs at Auburn University. An award winning teacher, he was named to the Who's Who in American Education in 2003. During his administrative tenure, Auburn's distance-based MBA program offerings have grown extensively, adding an Executive MBA in 1998, a Physician's Executive MBA in 1999, and a custom corporate MBA program for Jostens in 2002. His work in education issues has been published in the *Journal of Economic Education* and the *Journal of Executive Education,* while his research on financial institutions has appeared in the *Review of Economics and Statistics,* the *Journal of Money, Credit, and Banking,* and the *Journal of Banking and Finance.*

Stephanie A. Hicks is a former student at Auburn University. She graduated with a degree in economics.

Charles O. Kroncke, Jr. is Assistant Professor of Economics at the College of Mount Saint Joseph (OH). Professor Kroncke served on the Higher Education

Quality Assessment Councils of Estonia (1996) and Latvia (1997-1998). His economic education scholarship has been published in the *Journal of Economics and Finance Education*, while his work in the area of labor and education economics has appeared in the *Journal of Labor Research, Economics of Transition* and *Economics of Education Review*.

Luther D. Lawson is Professor of Economics at the University of North Carolina at Wilmington. He currently serves as Editor of the *Journal of Economics and Finance Education*.

Melody Lo is an Assistant Professor of Economics at The University of Southern Mississippi. She is a three-time recipient (1999, 2000 and 2001) of the Purdue Krannert Graduate School of Management Outstanding Graduate Student Instructor Award. Professor Lo's recent research interests concentrate on the speculative behavior of market makers in financial markets, inflation expectations formation in open economies, and government intervention policies toward exchange rates. She has published papers in the *Journal of International Money and Finance* and *Applied Financial Economics*.

Meghan Millea is an Associate Professor of Economics at Mississippi State University. Professor Millea is a recipient of the Bingham Fellowship (1997), an award for excellence in teaching at the University of Nebraska, the Mortar Board Professor of Eminence Award (2000), and the Thomas W. Hinkle Outstanding Undergraduate Teaching Award (2003) at Mississippi State University. Her research in the area of economic education has appeared in the *Journal of Economic Education, Journal of Economics and Economic Education Research* and the *College Student Journal*, while her research in labor and public economics has been published in the *Journal of Labor Research, International Journal of Business and Economics*, and *International Advances in Economic Research*.

Robert E. Niebuhr is Dean of the College of Business at Tennessee Technological University. Professor Niebuhr is the recipient of a 2003 Innovations Award from the Tennessee Board of Regents for the initiation of the Distance MBA Program at Tennessee Technological University. His research in the field of management has appeared in *The Academy of Management Journal, Journal of Management*, and the *Journal of Vocational Behavior*.

W. Charles Sawyer is the Partnership Society Professor of Economics at The University of Southern Mississippi. He is a coauthor of *International Economics*

(2nd edition, Prentice Hall, 2005) with Richard Sprinkle, and the recipient of the Graduate Business Association's Faculty of the Year Award (2003) and Faculty Excellence Award (1999). His work in the area of economic education has been published in the *Journal of Education for Business*, while his research in international and regional economics has been published in *Review of Economics and Statistics*, *Journal of Regional Science*, and the *Canadian Journal of Economics*.

William S. Schaninger is a Senior Project Manager with McKinsey & Co. His work focuses primarily on large scale organizational change, sustainability in operational improvements, and strategic HR. While at Auburn University, Bill worked with the leadership team in the College of Business to help create and launch the Executive MBA program for physicians.

Kenneth Smith is Assistant Professor of Economics at Millersville University (PA). Professor Smith served on the Higher Education Quality Assessment Councils of Estonia (1996-97) and Latvia (1997-2000), and worked as a consultant for the World Bank on a report examining economic education reform in the Baltic States. His research in the field of labor economics has been published in *Economics of Transition* and the *Baltic Journal of Economics*.

Lynnette Smyth is Associate Professor of Economics at Gordon College (GA). Professor Smyth's accomplishments as an economics educator extend back to her graduate school days, where she was named outstanding Teaching Assistant in the Statistics Department at the University of Missouri in the late 1980s, and she became the first doctoral student utilized to teach econometrics at Rutgers University in the early 1990s. More recently, she helped to organize the "Teaching Matters" Conference at Gordon College in the Spring of 2002 and 2003. Her work in the field of economic education has appeared in the *Journal of Economics and Finance Education*. Professor Smyth's research in the area of academic dishonesty has been published by the *Journal of Business Ethics* and the *Community College Review*.

Richard L. Sprinkle is a Professor of Economics at the University of Texas at El Paso. He is coauthor of *International Economics* (2nd edition, Prentice Hall, 2005) with W. Charles Sawyer. Professor Sprinkle received the Outstanding Graduate Professor of the Year Award in 1994, and the Outstanding Economics and Finance Professor of the Year Award in 1995. His work in the area of economic education has been published in the *Journal of Education for Business*, while his research in international and regional economics has been published in *Review of*

Economics and Statistics, Weltwirtschaftliches Archiv, and the *Journal of Regional Science.*

Len J. Treviño is Assistant Professor of Management at Washington State University. His recent research in business education has been published in the *Journal of Education for Business.* Outside of business education, he has published articles on international management in the *Journal of International Business Studies, International Business Review,* and the *Journal of World Business.*

Kamal P. Upadhyaya is Associate Professor of Economics at the University of New Haven (CT). Professor Upadhyaya is a former Ford Foundation Scholar (1982-84), and his research in the field of international economics has appeared in *Economics Letters,* the *International Trade Journal,* and the *Journal of Development Studies.*

Michael C. Withers is a Research Associate/Adjunct Faculty member at Mississippi State University in Meridian (MS). His research outside of the area of economic education deals mainly with labor economics issues.

M.C. Sunny Wong is Assistant Professor of Economics at The University of Southern Mississippi. He was a nominee for the Mortar Board Professor Award at the University of Oregon (2001) and the recipient of the Department Teaching Award at the University of Oregon (2002). Professor Wong's work on macroeconomics/monetary policy has been published by the *Journal of Macroeconomics* and *Political Research Quarterly.*

Foreword

Economic education, an area of economics that few scholars have chosen to investigate in the past, has now become an area of considerable importance. Many who teach undergraduate economics have begun to realize that research in economic pedagogy, techniques, strategies, and applications have more immediate and direct value than many abstract models presented at professional meetings and found in specialized journals.

Professional national (and regional) organizations like the American Economic Association, the Eastern Economic Association, and the Western Economic Association permit scholars to share their research by including multiple sessions in economic education. The upshot of this is that these organizations have now endorsed the legitimacy of this unique area for scholarly research, and that attendance at these sessions is burgeoning.

The following eleven essays reflect a broad area of economic education inquiry ranging from teaching assessment to the philosophy of the classroom. These articles represent but a small sample of the growing commentary among academics that place effective teaching as an important but unappreciated priority. Enjoy!

Luther D. Lawson
Editor
Journal of Economics and Finance Education

Part I.

Research

1

Student Evaluation of Teaching Scores in Economics
The Role of Student Metacognition

PAUL W. GRIMES AND MEGHAN J. MILLEA

I. Introduction

Every academic year, more than a million American college students take a Principles of Economics course. Significantly fewer will pursue the study of economics beyond this introductory level, and far fewer will decide to make economics their major. Academic economists have long recognized these facts and often lament their courses' poor reputation with students. Frequently, economics professors rationalize their plight by pointing to their discipline's heavy reliance on graphical and mathematical techniqes and suggest that this gives students the impression that economics must be a rigorous and difficult subject to master. The perception that students view economics as *hard* is often used to "explain" why student evaluation of teaching (SET) scores in the Principles of Economics course are often relatively low when compared to the scores from introductory courses in other social science and business disciplines. However, empirical research suggests that the determination of SET scores is a complex process with many variables coming into play (see for example, Marsh and Dunkin, 1992) including the reaction of students to the pedagogy of instruction. Noting that most academic economists continue to rely heavily on the "talk and chalk" (Becker and Watts, 1996) lecture method of instruction, Grimes (2002) recently suggested that student dissatisfaction with economics courses may reflect unmet expectations about learning and grades.

Specifically, Grimes examined the metacognitive ability of Principles students to assess their own learning by predicting future performance on an examination. His results revealed a significant prevalence and degree of student overconfidence which persisted over time. Given this, Grimes postulated that when students eventually realize that they have not reached their expected grade, dissatisfaction with their performance will manifest in relatively poor teaching evaluation scores. Furthermore, Grimes (2002) suggested that the standard lecture method of instruction breeds overconfidence because students generally do not receive significant feedback on the actual progress of their learning; such feedback is often limited to their scores on only a few major exams.

This paper extends Grimes' previous work by examining his proposition that a student's metacognitive ability to assess learning and grades is an important determinant of SET scores in the Principles of Economics. The next section outlines the research setting and describes the collection of data for analysis. This is followed by a presentation of the empirical model and results. The paper concludes with a review of the major findings and suggestions for future research.

2. Research Setting and Data Collection

This study was conducted at Mississippi State University (MSU), a Land Grant institution enrolling approximtely 16,500 students. MSU offers a full range of academic programs from the bachelor degree to the doctorate. Currently, MSU enrolls students from all 50 states and from more than 70 foreign nations. During the semester in which this study took place, entering first-year students had a mean ACT composite score of 23.5. African Americans made up about 18% of the student body which was also 53% male (reflecting the engineering and agricultural emphasis of a Land Grant school). In many ways, MSU is representative of large state-supported universities in the United States and, therefore, our results should be generalizable to a larger population.

The sample consisted of 149 students who were enrolled in a large auditorium section of a Principles of Macroeconomics course during a regular 16-week semester. At MSU, this course is the first in a traditional two-course Principles sequence offered by the economics faculty in the College of Business and Industry. As elsewhere, many of the students who take the Principles sequence at MSU are business majors, but the courses also service students from degree programs in arts and sciences, engineering, agriculture and life sciences, and others. Students from all majors may elect to take the Principles courses to satisfy the university's core requirements for the social sciences. Thus, our sample is fairly representative of the overall undergraduate student body.

Students in the sample were given three regular tests throughout the term and a final comprehensive exam during the last week of the semester. To gauge and measure each student's metacognitive ability to assess their personal course performance, students were asked to predict their score on the third regular test. Predictions were measured twice, once two days before the test and again on test day immediately prior to administering the test. Predictions were also measured in two ways; once by asking the students to predict the score (0–100%) they would receive on the third test, and once by asking them if they would perform better or worse on the third test when compared to their score on the last test taken in the course. An incentive scheme, which awarded a sliding scale of "bonus points" based on predictive accuracy, was employed to encourage serious predictions.[1] In addition, students completed a brief demographic questionnaire and a short student evaluation of teaching instrument prior to taking the third test. All mandated federal protocols concerning informed consent of the student subjects were followed and all data collection procedures were approved by the MSU Internal Review Board (IRB).

The accuracy of student expectations were measured by comparing each student's pre-test predictions to the test scores actually achieved. Table 1 provides a summary of these measurements. As seen in this table, two days prior to the test, the mean score predicted by the class as a whole was approximately 84%. Studying over the two days before the exam appears to have had a minimal effect on tempering student expectations as the mean prediction fell by only about two percentage points to roughly 82%. The actual class mean for the third test was only 78%. The same pattern is found but with a stronger magnitude when the students' relative predictions are examined. Two days before the test about 68% of the students predicted that their test score would rise, but immediately prior to taking the test only 62% of the students predicted they would improve on their last performance. In reality, only 43% of the students scored higher on test three than test two. Thus, when student predictions are compared to the actual scores achieved, as a class, students clearly over-predicted their true performance. This is true from both the absolute and relative perspectives.

Table 1

Student Expectations and Performance on Examination: Class Means and Standard Deviations by Gender

| | Expectations | | Performance |
	48-hours	Pre-test	Score
Total (N = 149)			
Student's score (%)	83.91	81.74	77.82
	(7.07)	(9.29)	(15.78)
% "Better" score	68.45[a]	61.74[a]	42.95[b]
	(0.47)	(0.49)	(0.49)
Males (N = 92)			
Student's score (%)	83.93	81.61	76.98
	(7.89)	(9.76)	(16.96)
% "Better" score	70.65[a]	63.04[a]	41.30[b]
	(0.45)	(0.48)	(0.49)
Females (N = 57)			
Student's score (%)	83.88	81.96	79.18
	(5.56)	(8.56)	(13.69)
% "Better" score	64.91[a]	59.65[a]	45.61[b]
	(0.48)	(0.49)	(0.50)

a: Percentage who expected to earn a midterm score higher than their score on the previous examination.

b: Percentage who actually earned a midterm score higher than their score on the previous examination.

Table 1 also reports the mean predictions and scores broken down across gender. The mean absolute predicted test scores for both men and women mirror those of the overall sample. However, female students actually scored, on average, about two points above their male counterparts resulting in a lesser degree of implied overconfidence for women. Even more interesting is divergence between men and women when their relative predictions are compared. When asked if they would perform better on the test, relative to past performance, significantly fewer women than men answered in the affirmative. While nearly 71% of the male students predicted a higher score two days prior to the test, only 65% of the female students did likewise. Though smaller, this gap persisted through the day of the test when 63% of the male students predicted better scores while only 60% of the female students believed they would achieve higher test scores. When these predictions are compared to the actual scores achieved, again the degree of over-confidence is smaller for women, due to both lower levels of expectations and higher mean levels of true performance.

3. The Empirical Model

The divergence between predicted test scores and actual test scores seen in Table 1 are consistent with the pattern of results reported earlier by Grimes (2002). He interpreted the observed positive gap between predicted performance and actual performance as a measure of student overconfidence resulting from inaccurate personal assessment of learning (poor metacognition). We adhered to that inter-pretation by including the presence of overconfidence as a determinant in a standard regression model of SET scores.[2] Our model took the following form:

$$(1)\ \mathbf{SET}_i = \alpha_i + \beta_{1i,j}\mathbf{M} + \beta_{2i,j}\mathbf{D} + \beta_{3i,j}\mathbf{A} + \varepsilon_i$$

where i reflects the students' evaluation of teaching score for the INSTRUC-TOR, the COURSE, and the OVERALL learning experience. **M** represents a vector of metacognitive measures, including the presence of overconfident stu-dent expectations, assumed to affect SET scores, **D** represents a vector of demo-graphic control variables, **A** represents a vector of academic student endowments and course performance variables. The α, βs, and ε are the standard ordinary least squares regression equation intercept, variable coefficients, and error term.

The specification of the variables included in each vector are reported in Table 2 along with their sample mean and standard deviation. The three dependent SET variables were constructed from responses to the SET form distributed prior to administration of the test.[3] The form required students to respond to a series of evaluation statements taken from a sample of instruments used at MSU and other universities. Each statement required students to respond using a Likert-type scale running from 1 = Strongly Disagree to 5 = Strongly Agree.[4] As seen in Table 2, the class means for the INSTRUCTOR, COURSE and OVERALL vari-ables are relatively high running from 3.9 to 4.4 on the 5-point scale. Thus, stu-dents in the class, on average were apparently well satisfied with their experience prior to administration of the third test.

Table 2
Specifications and Descriptive Statistics of Variables

Label	Specification	Mean	S.D.
Dependent Variables			
INSTRUCTOR	Student's mean score of instructor-based items on student evaluation of teaching instrument. Scale running from 1 = Strongly Disagree to 5 = Strongly Agree.	4.406	0.571
COURSE	Student's mean score of course-based items on student evaluation of teaching instrument. Scale running from 1 = Strongly Disagree to 5 = Strongly Agree.	3.921	0.540
OVERALL	Student's mean score of all items on student evaluation of teaching instrument. Scale running from 1 = Strongly Disagree to 5 = Strongly Agree.	4.244	0.536
Metacognition Measures			
OVERCONFIDENCE	1 = Student's pre-test expected score > exam score achieved; 0 = otherwise.	0.644	0.480
PREDICTIVE CALIBRATION	(Exam score achieved–pre-test expected score)^2/pre-test expected score.	2.40	4.139
Demographic Characteristics			
AGE	Student's age in years.	20.544	2.094
MALE	1 = Male student; 0 = female student.	0.617	0.488
BLACK	1 = Black student; 0 = white student.	0.262	0.441
Academic Endowments			
ACT	Student's reported composite score on the American College Test.	21.765	4.387
GPA	Student's cumulative college grade point average; standard 4-point scale.	2.667	0.605
REQUIRED	1 = Course specifically required in student's curriculum; 0 = course taken as an elective.	0.114	0.319

Course Performance			
DIVERGENCE	Difference between first exam score and class average score expressed as a percentage [(Student's Score - Class Avg.)/Class Avg.)×100].	0.316	0.221

Examination of the sample means for the independent variables reported in Table 2 provide a profile of the overall class. Consistent with Grimes' (2002) earlier student, a majority of the students demonstrated OVERCONFIDENCE. In fact, 64.4% of the class predicted a test score which exceeded the score actually earned. PREDICTIVE CALIBRATION reflects a measure of accuracy in student predictions about performance. The specification follows the functional form first put forth by Lichtenstein and Fischhoff (1977) which has become standard in the empirical metacognition literature. Smaller values of the PREDICTIVE CALIBRATION variable represent greater degrees of accuracy. The 2.4 mean for our sample suggests that the degree of inaccuracy in student predictions was relatively small. (For example, Grimes reported a PREDICTIVE CALIBRATION mean of 4.3 for his sample of Principles students).

The means for the demographic variables indicate that the sample was somewhat more male than female and included a relatively large number of African American students (about 26% compared to 18% for the overall MSU student body). The average student age of 20.54 years is well within the range often reported for Principles of Economics students nationwide. Looking at the academic endowment and course performance variables, the sample's mean ACT score of 21.77 is not significantly different from the overall university mean. The mean GPA of 2.67 indicates that the class, on average, earns a typical C+ overall. Interestingly, only about 11% of the students reported that they were required to take the course, but 65% had taken a course in economics before, either in high school or in college. The DIVERGENCE variable was included in the model to control for students' relative course performance and its sample mean reflects a measure of the spread of scores across the class.

4. Results

Equation (1) was estimated using standard OLS techniques. Results for the INSTRUCTOR, COURSE, and OVERALL specifications of the equation are reported in Table 3. For each specification, a significant F-statistic and an acceptable cross-sectional R^2 was obtained. Most of the regression coefficients obtained their expected sign and many were also found to be statistically significant.

Table 3
OLS Regression Results: Determinants of Student Evaluation of Teaching Scores

Variable	INSTRUCTOR	COURSE	OVERALL
CONSTANT	3.127***	3.399***	3.218***
	(4.989)	(5.654)	(5.504)
AGE	0.022	0.004	0.016
	(0.997)	(0.175)	(0.773)
MALE	-0.178*	-0.161*	-0.172*
	(1.867)	(1.766)	(1.940)
BLACK	0.063	-0.036	0.030
	(0.547)	(0.328)	(0.278)
ACT	0.007	0.002	0.005
	(0.570)	(0.147)	(0.457)
GPA	0.224**	0.134	0.194**
	(2.271)	(1.417)	(2.109)
REQUIRED	-0.251*	-0.208*	-0.237*
	(1.807)	(1.697)	(1.829)
DIVERGENCE	0.006**	0.007***	0.007***
	(2.349)	(2.869)	(2.662)
OVERCONFIDENCE	0.304**	0.290***	0.299***
	(2.764)	(2.751)	(2.918)
PREDICTIVE CALIBRATION	-0.001	-0.003	-0.001
	(0.009)	(0.241)	(0.089)
Adjusted R^2	0.148	0.123	0.157
F-statistic	3.860	3.300	4.060

()–Absolute value of t statistic.

*** Statistically significant at the 0.01 level, two-tailed test. ** Statistically significant at the 0.05 level, two-tailed test. * Statistically significant at the 0.10 level, two-tailed test.

Of the three demographic control variables, only the coefficients for the MALE variable were statistically significant across all three specifications. The negative sign indicates that, holding all else constant, male students provided significantly lower scores across the SET statements designed to evaluate the instructor, the course, and the overall learning experience. Given that the course was taught by a female professor, this finding is not unexpected. The SET literature suggests that students evaluate like-gendered instructors more favorably (Basow and Spielberg, 1987). Thus, female students are likely to more highly rate female professors and male students are more likely to highly rate male professors. The current results are consistent with this phenomenon.

Examination of the academic endowment and course performance variables reveals that the coefficient of GPA was found to be positive and statistically significant in the INSTRUCTOR and OVERALL specifications in the model. Thus, students with relatively stronger academic histories of performance provided more positive SET scores, *ceteris paribus*, along these two dimensions. The REQUIRED coefficient was found to be negative and significant across all three specifications. This indicates that students who did not independently choose to take the Principles of Macroeconomics course reported less satisfaction across the board. The positive and significant DIVERGENCE coefficient, appearing in all three specifications of the model, indicate that students clustered about the class mean. Thus, the farther above the class mean a student rises, the higher the value of the expected SET score. Each of the results for the academic endowment and course performance variables are consistent with previous empirical studies of the determination of SET scores.

Turning to the coefficients for the metacognition variables, Table 3 reveals that the PREDICTIVE CALIBRATION coefficient never obtained statistical significance in any of the three specifications of the model. Thus, the degree of accuracy in a student's self-assessment of performance does not appear to be related to the determination of SET scores, all else being the same. However, the coefficients for the OVERCONFIDENCE variable are positive and statistically significant, using a two-tailed test, across the three specifications. Therefore, students who overestimated their true test performance provided significantly higher SET scores for the INSTRUCTOR, the COURSE, and their OVERALL classroom experience, *ceteris paribus*.

At first glance, this finding appears to run counter to Grimes' (2002) proposition that low SET scores will result when overconfidence, resulting from inaccurate self-assessment of learning, generates dissatisfaction when students realize that their expectations have not been met. However, this sequence of events requires students to be confronted with evidence of their overconfidence. This would naturally occur when students receive their final course grade, or at the point in the semester when additional improvements in performance will no longer significantly affect their final course grade. Thus, any dissatisfaction from unmet expectations will most likely occur at, or near, the end of the course term. In our experimental design, SET scores were obtained well before the end of the semester when such dissatisfaction is most likely to be observed. It is not surprising then to find that overconfidence was associated with higher SET scores—the disappointment of unmet expectations had yet to occur. In fact, to the contrary, it appears that overconfidence generated a sense of optimism in students which translated into positive evaluations of the instructor and course.

The current results cannot rule out the relationship between student over-confidence and low SET scores as postulated by Grimes (2002). A true test requires comparison of student expectations measured during the course with SET scores obtained after distribution of final grades to the class. Until such studies are completed, we cannot reject the hypothesized relationship between metacognitive functioning and student satisfaction.

5. Conclusions

Using a sample of students enrolled in a large auditorium section of a Principles of Macroeconomics course, we examined the relationship between students' self-assessment of performance and student evaluation of teaching scores. Students in the sample demonstrated a significant propensity to overestimate their future per-formance on a regular examination. A standard regression model of SET scores was estimated which included the presence/absence of overconfidence as an explanatory variable. The results indicated that students who overestimated their personal performance provided significantly higher SET scores for the instructor, the course, and for the overall class experience. Given that the evaluation proce-dures occurred prior to the determination of final grades, the results cannot be used to reject Grimes' (2002) hypothesis that unmet expectations, expressed as overconfidence in the self-assessment of personal performance, leads to dissatis-faction and lowers student evaluation scores.

Do the current results provide any useful information for instructors of intro-ductory economics courses? Yes, on at least two points. First, our data provide additional evidence that students in typical lecture hall principles courses are often overconfident in their expectations about course performance. This suggests that instructors need to provide more, or better, feedback to students concerning their grades so that students can form more realistic expectations. The importance of this cannot be overlooked since it is likely that overconfidence results in fewer study hours and other negative behavior on the part of students. Second, from an instructor's perspective, the current findings indicate that if students are overconfident in their performance expectations, higher SET scores may be obtained by conducting the evaluation *prior* to the determination of final grades. In practice, most schools follow procedures whereby evaluations are con-ducted at the end of the term when dissatisfaction with unmet expectations is most likely to occur. If higher evaluation scores are the objective, then the timing of the evaluation may be important when overconfidence and unmet expectations exist. Of course, an additional benefit of earlier evaluations is that the instructor may have time to make changes in the course based on student feedback.

Additional research is necessary to fully understand how the metacognitive functions of college students affect their behavior and perceptions of instructors and courses. In particular, empirical research is needed to determine how over-confidence affects students' study habits and course preparation activity. Pedagogical research is also needed to determine how instructors can organize and teach courses in ways that yield realistic expectations of performance and encourage productive study habits.

Notes

* The authors extend their thanks to all of the college students who participated in this study and to Stephanie Henson for her help in data collection and data-base development. Marybeth Grimes provided expert editorial assistance.

1. Details concerning this bonus point scheme are available upon request of the authors along with copies of the survey and informed consent release forms.

2. For examples of other OLS regression-based models of SET score determination in college courses, see Lumsdem (1973), Cohen (1981), and Millea and Grimes (2002).

3. Copies of the complete SET form are available upon request of the authors.

4. Given the ordinal nature of the dependent variable, our model could also be estimated using a multinomial ordered probit technique. Specification tests revealed that the results were comparable with the OLS estimates which are reported here for the ease of exposition and interpretation.

References

Basow, S.A. and N.T. Silberg (1987) "Student evaluations of college professors: Are female and male professors rated differently?" *Journal of Educational Psychology* 79: 308-314.

Becker, W.E. and M. Watts (1996) "Chalk and talk: A national survey of teaching undergraduate economics," *American Economic Review* 86: 448-454.

Cohen, P.A. (1981) "Student ratings of instruction and student achievement: A meta-analysis of multisection validity studies," *Review of Educational Research* 51: 281-308.

Grimes, P.W. (2002) "The overconfident principles of economics student: An examination of metacognitive skill," *Journal of Economic Education* 33: 15-30.

Lichtenstein, S. and B. Fischhoff (1977) "Do those who know more also know more about how much they know?" *Organizational Behavior and Human Performance* 20: 159-183.

Lumsdem, K.G. (1973) "Analysis of student evaluations of faculty and courses," *Journal of Economic Education* 5: 54-56.

Marsh, H.W. and M. Dunkin (1992) "Students' evaluations of university teaching: A multi-dimensional perspective," in J.C. Smart (Editor), *Higher education: Handbook of theory and research*, New York, NY: Agathon Press, pp. 143-233.

Millea, M.J. and P.W. Grimes (2002) "Grade expectations and student evaluation of teaching," *College Student Journal* 36: 582-590.

2

Getting Econometrics Students to Evaluate Student Evaluations

KENNETH SMITH

I. Introduction

Student evaluations of faculty are almost universal at American colleges and universities. Frequently they play a central role in overall faculty evaluations concerning such issues as tenure, promotion, and compensation. While considerable empirical work exists in the psychology literature concerning the validity of student evaluation (see Cashin, 1995, for an extensive overview), empirical analysis on student evaluations conducted by economists is more scarce (though some certainly exist, including Krautmann and Sander, 1999; Boex, 2000; and Bosshardt and Watts, 2001). Further, while students certainly have some insight into how their peers rate professors at their own school, their insight into the general evaluation process is probably even more limited.

A web site that has attracted considerable publicity and interest, ratemyprofessors.com, provides a standardized source of data to explore various aspects of student evaluations of faculty. Additionally, use of a data set assembled with data from ratemyprofessors.com actually seems to enhance student interest in applying econometrics in an introductory undergraduate course and getting them to think a bit about how professors are evaluated by students.

2. The Data

As mentioned, the faculty rating data were gathered from ratemyprofessors.com. This web site is freely accessible, and anyone can rate a professor. Thus, the data are clearly not gathered in a scientific manner. However, the web site does represent a standardized rating system that can be compared across different schools or schools representing different institutional types (e.g., liberal arts colleges or comprehensive universities). It has also clearly attracted the interest of a great number of students and so represents a means of getting students interested in data analysis, and perhaps getting them to think more about the faculty evaluation process.

The data used for the statistical analyses were primarily gathered in January of 2003. Individual faculty represent the unit of observation (Table 2 provides definitions of all relevant variables). An individual faculty member was placed in the sample if he or she had received ten or more student ratings.[1] The web site was essentially scoured for all faculty with ten or more ratings. A few schools have hundreds of faculty with ten or more ratings. In such cases, a random subset (up to 200 faculty) was chosen. The final sample includes 2,986 faculty from 82 different schools. Data on the selectivity, cost, and institutional type of the various colleges and universities represented in the sample are taken from *U.S. News and World Report America's Best Colleges* (2003 edition).

Faculty are included in the sample only if their subject area was discernable from the ratings. In almost all cases, students include either the subject the faculty teaches or the course number. Though no attempt was made to sort evaluations by lower level, upper level, and graduate courses, it is clear that almost all rankings come from undergraduate students, and they appear to be fairly heavily concentrated in introductory level courses in virtually all subject categories.

3. Statistical Analysis

Table 1 presents descriptive statistics from the sample. The mean values for the quality variables are consistent with what most would predict. Students at liberal arts colleges have the highest mean satisfaction level for both the *helpfulness* of their professors and the *clarity* of the classroom presentation. Comprehensive schools have a slightly higher *quality* mean than Ph.D. granting institutions (henceforth referred to as research institutions) primarily due to a higher helpfulness score. These results, and subsequent regression results, are broadly consistent with empirical findings on faculty incentives and time allocation at various types of educational institutions (Singell et al., 1996). There is virtually no overall *quality* rating differential between public and private schools. Mean values for

Table 1
Descriptive Statistics Mean Values (standard deviations)[1,2]

	Pooled Sample	Libarts	Comp.	Ph.D.	Public	Private
help	3.529 (0.956)	3.705 (0.903)	3.533 (0.950)	3.489 (0.970)	3.536 (0.952)	3.514 (0.966)
clear	3.445 (0.981)	3.629 (0.934)	3.426 (0.974)	3.428 (0.996)	3.437 (0.983)	3.461 (0.976)
quality	3.490 (0.956)	3.666 (0.905)	3.484 (0.949)	3.461 (0.970)	3.490 (0.954)	3.491 (0.959)
sexy	0.059 (0.156)	0.088 (0.180)	0.050 (0.143)	0.063 (0.165)	0.050 (0.144)	0.078 (0.179)
ease	3.025 (0.821)	2.861 (0.748)	3.007 (0.840)	3.081 (0.807)	3.056 (0.821)	2.954 (0.818)
select	3.287 (0.590)	3.746 (0.471)	3.149 (0.595)	3.360 (0.544)	3.200 (0.590)	3.482 (0.544)
cost	9.417 (7.995)	19.312 (9.662)	7.689 (6.442)	9.483 (7.835	4.391 (1.345)	20.812 (4.189)
N	2,986	256	1,512	1,218	2,072	914

Notes:
1. The data for ease, help, clear, quality, and sexy were collected from ratemyprofessors.com (used with the permission of the founder/president of the web site, John Swapceinski). Data on selectivity, cost, and institutional type are from *U.S. News and World Report America's Best Colleges* (2003 edition). Variable definitions are provided in Table 2.
2. A list of schools and sample sizes for each school are available upon request.

selectivity and *cost* are also consistent with standard expectations. Liberal arts schools (all but one in the sample are private) are more selective and more costly on average than are comprehensive or research universities. Private schools also have a higher mean selectivity rating and cost nearly five times as much on average as public schools in the sample. There are also notable differences regarding *ease* ratings with liberal arts faculty having the lowest mean easiness rating and faculty at research institutions the highest. There are also differences in the perceived *sexual appeal* of faculty across institutional types, with faculty at liberal arts and private institutions faring relatively well and faculty at public and comprehensive institutions fairing relatively poorly.

Table 2
Variable Definitions

Variable	Variable Definition
help	Students are coached as follows: "Is the teacher approachable and nice? Is he rude, arrogant, or just plain mean? Is he willing to help after class?" help=1 to 5 from least to most helpful.
clear	Students are coached as follows: "How well does the teacher convey the class topics? Is he clear in his presentation? Is he organized and does he use class time effectively?" clear=1 to 5 from least to most clear.
quality	The average scores for help help and clear. quality=1 to 5 from lowest to highest quality.
sexy	The proportion of students who rate a professor as sexy (the options are simply sexy or not). sexy=0 to 1.
sexy×ease	An interaction term multiplying the sexy and ease scores for a faculty member.
select	A measure of school selectivity employed by *U.S. News and World Report America's Best Colleges*. The selectivity measure is weighted composite of: entrance exam (SAT or ACT) score (weight=0.40), high school class ranking (proportion in top 10 or 25 percent of class; weight=0.35), school acceptance rate (weight=0.15), and proportion of accepted students who choose to attend the school (weight=0.10). School selectivity (along with numeric score) is ranked as: least selective (1), less selective (2), selective (3), more selective (4), and most selective (5).
cost	Tuition cost in thousands of dollars. For public schools, in-state tuition is reported.
public	1 if the school is a public institution, and 0 if it is private.
libarts	1 if the school is a liberal arts college, 0 otherwise (*U.S. News and World Report America's Best Colleges* classifications are used here and for subsequent institutional classifications).
comprehensive	1 if the school is a comprehensive university, 0 otherwise.
phd	1 if the school is a university granting a range of doctoral degrees, 0 otherwise.
subject controls	Professors are categorized into 26 different disciplines according to the classification used by ratemyprofessors.com.

The Assigned Regressions

This data set was used for a problem set to complement the material in Chapter 6 of Jeffrey Wooldridge's *Introductory Econometrics* textbook (2000) that includes a section on the use of interaction terms in OLS regression. Students were asked to run the following regressions:

(1) $quality = \beta_0 + \beta_1 sexy + \beta_2 ease + \varepsilon,$

(2) $quality = \beta_0 + \beta_1 sexy + \beta_2 ease + \beta_3 [sexy \times ease] + \varepsilon.$

Columns two and three of Table 3 present the results of regressions (1) and (2). The regression (1) results are fairly straightforward and students were able to interpret the results fairly easily. I find students have a difficult time with interaction terms and that was the case here as well. A notable difference with this assignment was the student level of interest regarding the results and the amount of discussion the results generated in class. In the end most students seemed to be comfortable with the quantifiable interpretation of results—even for regression (2).

As the second column of Table 3 indicates, a one point increase in a professor's sexiness rating increases his or her predicted quality score by about 1.48 points—a substantial amount on a 1 to 5 scale. Since the sexiness score is measured as a proportion of students who ranked a faculty member as sexy, the sexiness score is on a zero-to-one scale. Thus, the result does have the somewhat subtle interpretation (not generally picked up by students initially) that if an individual student considers a faculty member to be sexy, it will have the predicted effect of increasing his or her overall quality rating of that faculty member by 1.48 points. Students tend to have no problem picking up the fact that this is extremely significant in a practical as well as statistical sense. In fact, regardless of model specification (some potential extensions are considered below), perceptions of sexual appeal tend to have an overpowering effect on faculty ratings, though the most common sexiness rating is zero (for a little over 80 percent of professors in the sample). Further, this result does not seem to surprise many students.

Table 3
OLS Results (dependent variable: quality)[1]

Variable	(A)	(B)	(C)	(D)
intercept	1.511***	1.386***	1.390***	1.305***
	(0.052)	(0.054)	(0.054)	(0.081)
sexy	1.478***	4.855***	4.853***	4.825***
	(0.089)	(0.435)	(0.435)	(0.431)
ease	0.626***	0.667***	0.667***	0.677***
	(0.017)	(0.018)	(0.018)	(0.018)
sexy×ease		-1.003***	-1.003***	-1.012***
		(0.127)	(0.127)	(0.126)
economics[2]			-0.057	
			(0.064)	
subject controls[3]	no	no	no	yes
F-statistic	947.41***	665.65***	499.40***	83.50***
R-squared	0.389	0.401	0.401	0.423

Notes:

1. Standard errors are given in parentheses. In this and the following table, *** denotes significance at the 1% level and ** denotes significance at the 5% level.
2. Economics is added as a dummy, so this estimate compares economics to all other subjects.
3. In this regression, economics was left out of the regression and serves as the reference subject.

The results further indicate that the perceived level of ease has a dramatic effect on a professor's quality rating. The results indicate that a one point increase in a professor's easiness score (also on a 1 to 5 scale) increases his or her predicted quality score by about 0.63 points—again a statistically and practically potent result. As with the sexiness result, students seemed comfortable with this finding. As a note, upon reflection, many students did seem a bit taken aback at the magnitude of both the sexiness and easiness results.

The introduction of the interaction term (multiplying the ease and sexy scores) adds an interesting twist. The results of regression (2) indicate that being perceived as sexy will have an enormous effect on a professor's quality rating if he or she is also perceived to be very difficult. The benefit of sexual appeal on the quality rating fades quickly as a professor becomes easier. Similarly, faculty who are not generally perceived as sexy will substantially increase their predicted quality score by being easier. However, as the proportion of students who find a professor sexy rises (at least to a point—a quite high point given sexiness ratings in the sample), the benefits of being perceived as easy fade away rather quickly.

A literal interpretation of the regression (2) results indicates the following: If a student gives a professor an ease rating of one (the most difficult), a positive sexiness rating boosts the professor's overall predicted quality score by almost 3.9 points. However, for a student who gives a professor an ease rating of five (the easiest), a positive sexiness rating leaves the overall predicted quality score essentially unchanged. Additionally, if a professor receives a sexiness score of zero, each added easiness point increases the predicted quality rating by two-thirds of a point. However, if two-thirds of a professor's students rate him or her as sexy, ease has no influence on the predicted quality score. Some students noted, with surprise, that literal interpretation of results also predicts that being easier will actually diminish one's quality rating if more than two-thirds of a professor's students rate him or her as sexy. This is a somewhat counterintuitive result. It may be due to the fact that the proportion of faculty with such a high sexiness score is negligible. Less than 1.5 percent of the sample can boast a sexiness score equal to or in excess of two-thirds.

In a qualitative sense, how can the interaction term be interpreted? In-class discussion centered around the fact that many students see both ease and sexual appeal as favorable qualities in a professor. Thus having one might make a lack of the other more forgivable. In other words, a good-looking professor can be forgiven for being difficult or an easy professor can be forgiven for lacking sexual appeal.

4. Some Potential Extensions

The sample includes faculty from 26 different subject categories. Thus, of obvious interest to economists and economics students is how do economics faculty rate relative to others? Columns (C) and (D) of Table 3 explore potential discipline differences. Column (C) compares economics to all other subjects lumped together. The results indicate no statistical difference in quality ratings between economists and all other faculty. Column (D) presents OLS results when a full range of subject dummies is added to the regression with economics serving as the reference subject. Overall, differences in student quality ratings across disciplines frequently disappear when control for ease is included.[2] Despite some substantial differences in mean quality scores across disciplines, only five of 25 disciplines have a statistically significant difference than economics in terms of quality. Four areas rank higher—sciences (at the 1% level), history (at the 5% level), and political science and psychology (at the 10% level). One subject, computer science, ranks lower (at the 1% level).

Table 4 provides regression results with statistically simple extensions that cover several issues of potential interest to educators, students, and economists. The issues that might be addressed in Table 4 include the effects of student attributes, institutional type, and tuition cost on subjective quality ratings.

A frequent issue that arises in econometrics is the effect of unobservable characteristics on regression results. Student attributes such as interest in study and natural ability are likely to affect faculty quality ratings. The inclusion of select (a

Table 4
OLS Results—Possible Extensions
Dependent Variable: quality

Variable	(A)	(B)	(C)	(D)
intercept	1.184***	1.182***	1.192***	1.133***
	(0.092)	(0.099)	(0.098)	(0.124)
sexy	4.834***	4.835***	4.734***	4.815***
	(0.435)	(0.435)	(0.433)	(0.435)
ease	0.666***	0.666***	0.672***	0.668***
	(0.017)	(0.018)	(0.017)	(0.018)
sexy×ease	-0.997***	-0.998***	-0.971***	-0.993***
	(0.126)	(0.127)	(0.126)	(0.127)
select	0.062***	0.062***	0.053***	
	(0.023)	(0.024)	(0.024)	
public	(0.030)	0.002	0.035	0.191**
		(0.031)	(0.091)	
libarts[1]			0.199***	
			(0.054)	
phd[1]			-0.090***	
			(0.029)	
cost				0.013**
				(0.005)
subject controls	no	no	no	no
F-statistic	502.13***	401.57***	294.52***	401.13***
R-squared	0.403	0.403	0.409	0.402

Note:
1. Comprehensive universities serve as the reference group.

measure of school selectivity) is a potential way to address this issue. The regression results in fact are consistent with the predicted effect. Controlling for the sexual appeal and perceived ease of a faculty member, students at more selective schools tend to give their professors higher quality ratings. Further, this result proves to be fairly robust to model specification, though as column (D) indicates, the result is somewhat weaker when controls for institutional type are included. This in itself provides a nice example when discussing multicollinearity as liberal arts college tend to be more selective than comprehensive or research universities in the sample, and liberal arts professors tend to have higher quality ratings.

The results concerning institutional type, vis-à-vis liberal arts, comprehensive, or research institution, are also consistent with prediction. Given the other controls present, students tend to be more satisfied with teaching quality at liberal arts institutions and less satisfied with teaching quality at research institutions relative to comprehensive universities. These differences are statistically significant and robust to other model specifications.

The results regarding quality ratings at public versus private schools might be more surprising. A common prediction would probably be that quality ratings would tend to be higher at private institutions. However, columns (C) and (D) of Table 4 indicate no statistical difference between overall predicted quality ratings at public and private institutions. In fact, when cost is controlled for (column (D) of Table 4), public institutions emerge looking like a bargain. These results indicate that controlling for cost, students at public institutions are actually significantly more satisfied with the quality of teaching than are students at private institutions. The results of column (D) also indicate that when it comes to teaching, money can buy satisfaction. However, while the coefficient on cost is statistically significant, it is practically rather small, indicating $10,000 buys about a 0.13 increase in overall faculty quality ratings at a particular school. Further, the statistical significance of cost is quite sensitive to model specification. For example, if selectivity is included in the regression in column (D), the cost coefficient remains positive but becomes insignificant (the selectivity coefficient is significant in this case).

5. Conclusion

Potential applications in an introductory econometrics course of a data set constructed using Internet-based student evaluations were explored above. The data from ratemyprofessors.com have two distinct advantages. First, they attract student interest and are successful in engaging students in basic multivariate OLS regression and OLS regression using an interaction term. Second, the results from the data are interesting in-and-of themselves. The results provide rather strong evidence (though data gathering methods can certainly be questioned) that the sexual appeal and perceived easiness of a professor have a strong positive influence on his or her student quality ratings. Since educators or educational administrators probably do not generally consider sexual appeal and ease desirable faculty characteristics, the results might also contribute to the debate concerning the efficacy of using student evaluations for the purpose of faculty performance review. The results presented above also provide rare evidence that institutional type and student attributes are important determinants of student evaluations of faculty.

Notes

1. Restricting the sample to faculty with ten or more ratings is empirically supported in the psychology literature (Cashin, 1995).

2. When controls for faculty ease are removed and only sexiness is controlled for, science and history faculty no longer have statistically better quality ratings than economics faculty, though faculty from five other subjects—communications, education, english, law and foreign languages—do receive statistically better quality ratings (in addition to political science and psychology). Computer science faculty alone continue to have statistically lower quality ratings than do economics faculty, though significance drops to the 5% level.

References

Boex, L.F.J. (2000) "Attributes of effective economics instructors: An analysis of student evaluations," *Journal of Economic Education* 31: 211-227.

Bosshardt, W. and M. Watts (2001) "Comparing student and instructor evaluations of teaching," *Journal of Economic Education* 32: 3-17.

Cashin, W.E. (1995) "Student ratings of teaching: The research revisited," Idea Paper No. 32, Kansas State University Center for Faculty Evaluation and Development.

Krautmann, A.C. (1999) "Grades and student evaluations of teachers," *Economics of Education Review* 18: 59-63.

Singell, L.D., Jr., J.H. Lillydahl, and L.D. Singell, Sr. (1996) "Will changing times change the allocation of faculty time?" *Journal of Human Resources* 31: 429-449.

U.S. News and World Report America's Best Colleges (2003 edition).

Wooldridge, J.M. (2000) *Introductory econometrics: A modern approach*, New York: Southwestern College Publishing.

3

Principles of Economics and the Reinforcement and Improvement of Math Skills

LYNNETTE SMYTH AND CHARLES O. KRONCKE, JR.

I. Introduction

There is general agreement among college level economics instructors that a strong background in mathematics has a positive influence on student performance in an economics course. The quantitative portion of this study examines the reverse—i.e., does taking a principles of economics class significantly impact student math skills? Math skills are unlike the skills required to ride a bicycle, they can become weaker and even forgotten if not used. Thus it is important for students to continually use the knowledge and techniques learned in the mathematics classroom if they are to retain and improve these skills.

Research shows that a student's background in mathematics is an important predictor of successful student outcomes in college-level coursework. Berry (2003) effectively demonstrates that students who take a course more rigorous than algebra two as part of their secondary education curriculum are more likely to place into and succeed in college algebra than their peers who did not take the more advanced high school course. In addition, it has also been shown that the educational benefits in any one college course are not solely confined to that particular discipline but may have spillover effects on student performance across disciplines. Ballard and Johnson (2004) have shown that skills learned in mathematics coursework spill over into the economics classroom. Milkman, McCoy, and Brassfield (1995) show that completing a business math sequence which includes introductory calculus has a positive and significant effect on student grades in both principles of macroeconomics and principles of microeconomics. On the other hand, they also conclude that their finding does not indicate that students learn more economics course content; rather, these students use their previously acquired math skills to simply spend less time studying for their principles courses. Kroncke and Smyth (2003) find that successful completion of a non remedial math course has a positive and significant effect on the grade of a quiz on indifference curve analysis. Thus there is evidence that good student math skills are associated with good student performance in economics coursework.

However, the spillover effect may move in both directions, i.e., skills learned in an economics classroom may improve math performance just as readily as skills learned in a mathematics classroom may improve performance in economics. Principles of economics is a course that utilizes already encountered but perhaps infrequently used skills such as basic math, fractions, graphing, and solving single equations for an unknown variable. Thus it is possible that such skills will be reinforced or indeed improved when a student is in an economics classroom. This direction of the spillover effect, from economics to mathematics, is of particular importance in the State of Georgia. The Board of Regents of the University System of Georgia currently requires all college students to pass a standardized examination of basic reading and writing skills in order to receive even a two-year college degree. In the past few years an initial effort has been made to allow the eventual inclusion of basic math skills as an element of the Regents' testing program, and thus college-level non-mathematics coursework that improves mathematical skills has become of increasing interest.

Certainly success in mathematics opens the door to a wide array of academic disciplines, and thus mathematics is an important part of higher education— hence the general education mathematics requirement for all students. But it can be tempting for faculty teaching non-math courses with mathematical elements (e.g., engineering, psychology, economics, business) to treat a student's set of math skills as a static variable that the student either does or does not possess upon initial enrollment in their courses. This research shows that student math skills are dynamic, and that economics can be utilized to develop these skills over the course of a semester.

This study contains six sections. After the introduction, a brief description of the students who participated in the research is given. In the third section, a detailed explanation of the research project is presented. In addition, the controls that were utilized to ensure that the research methods used were scientific are discussed. The fourth section contains a presentation of the demographic and descriptive statistics of the sample set. The empirical techniques and results are found in the fifth section. The conclusion contains a summary of some of the more interesting findings and implications of the study.

2. The Students

A total of 258 students from 20 sections of principles of macroeconomics and principles of microeconomics at Gordon College participated in this research project in the Fall semester of 2001 and the Spring semester of 2002. Gordon College is a two-year college that grants associate degrees and is part of the University System of Georgia. The majority of the students subsequently transfer these credits to four-year schools in the State of Georgia. Gordon College is different from many two-year colleges in that it provides residential living for its students, and approximately twenty percent of the student body lives on campus. The students come both from the suburbs of Atlanta and Macon and from the surrounding rural areas of central Georgia. Most of the students surveyed are either business transfer majors or are students from other disciplines fulfilling a social science requirement.

3. The Project

Principle of macroeconomics and microeconomics are not sequenced at Gordon College and are not on the list of approved courses for students that are required to take remedial math courses; thus students in the principles courses have demonstrated at least a minor level of mathematical proficiency. All economics instructors at Gordon College used the same textbooks and there was no faculty turnover during the time period of this study.

The students were given a math skills quiz in the first and last weeks of each semester. There were fourteen weeks between the two quizzes. The quizzes were not returned to or discussed with the students, and they were never told the correct answers. Quiz scores were not part of the students' course grades. All quizzes tested the same mathematical concepts, but the numbers used in the problems differed for each quiz and the order in which the concepts were tested changed with each quiz. Quiz dates were not announced in advance, thus students were unable to study outside of class. In addition, at the beginning of the semester, students were not told that they would be quizzed again at the end of the semester.

The average class size for principles of economics was about 30 students per course. Because the study required paired data, only those students who completed both the quiz at the beginning of the semester and at the end of the semester were included in the project. Thus students who added the course after the first week and students who were absent on the quiz date either at the beginning or at the end of the semester were not included. Regular class attendance was not required by either instructor.

If a student participated in the study in both semesters, only the first semester's quiz results were used. If a student was simultaneously enrolled in both economics courses in the same semester, only the quiz results from the macroeconomics class were included in the study. Only a few students fell into either of the above noted categories, and thus very few quiz results were excluded.

The quiz tested a variety of mathematical concepts that a student should recall from prior academic experience and should be exposed to in a semester-long economics course. The concepts tested included word problems, percentages, finding the slope of a line from a graph, positive and negative relationships, absolute values, recognition of a point of tangency between a line and a curve, and basic algebra including solving single equations for unknown variables. See Appendix 1 for a sample quiz.

Additionally, an extensive background survey was gathered for each student. This survey provides information about a student's intelligence, preparation, attitude, effort, and demographic characteristics (Park and Kerr, 1990). To measure intelligence we collected the student's self-reported cumulative college GPA and whether the respondent had ever attended a four-year institution. Since Gordon College is a two year institution within a state university system, some of our students have the necessary standardized test scores to be admitted from high school to four-year institutions but then failed to perform satisfactorily at these institutions. Thus, prior attendance at a four-year institution is a variable of interest.

Several variables were gathered to measure a student's level of preparation. These include dummy variables for taking high school economics, high school geometry, and a higher level high school math course (trigonometry, precalculus, or calculus). Also, dummy variables were created for successful completion of a college level economics class and of a college level non-remedial math course. To measure attitude we included a dummy variable for whether or not the student's choice of academic major requires the current economics course. This variable may indicate the student's perceived value of the course.

In order to measure student effort, a number of variables were collected. These include the student's estimate of the number of weekly hours participating in college related extracurricular activities, the number of semester hours of course work in the current semester, and the self-reported number of absences in the current economics course. In addition we created dummy variables for whether or not the respondent is employed, currently has financial aid, and has ever lost financial aid due to poor grades. Our demographic variables include age, sex, parental formal education levels, and residence in a college dormitory.

The project goal is to investigate whether there has been a significant improvement in math skills over the semester; thus, it is important to collect information on what courses other than economics the student is simultaneously taking that may also develop math skills. We created a dummy variable for whether or not the student is currently enrolled in any accounting course and a dummy variable whether or not the student is currently enrolled in a college level math course. To control for possible variation between the two semesters, we tracked which semester the respondent participated in the project. In addition we noted which of the two faculty members was the student's instructor.

4. Descriptive Statistics

The results of the background survey of respondents are presented in Table 1 and Appendix 2. Basic demographic statistics (Table 1) show that approximately 52% of the participating students are female, the average student age is 20.13 years, and roughly 21% of the students reside in campus housing, a figure that is consistent with the college-wide residency rate. Almost 30% of the respondents

Table 1
Demographic Statistics

Average Age	20.13 years
Gender (% female)	52%
Residence in a dormitory	21.4%
Currently employed	70.0%
Dad's Highest Education Level	
Did not complete high school	5.8%
Completed high school	25.6
Attended some college but did not finish	18.6
Completed an undergraduate degree	17.1
Completed graduate/professional school	12.8
Unsure	6.2
No response	13.9
Total	100.0%
Mom's Highest Education Level	
Did not complete high school	6.2%
Completed high school	28.7
Attended some college but did not finish	18.6
Completed an undergraduate degree	14.7
Completed graduate/professional school	15.9
Unsure	3.1
No response	12.8
Total	100.0%

report that their fathers completed an undergraduate degree or higher with an additional 18.6% reporting that their fathers had attended some college. Similarly, 30.6% of the students have mothers who completed an undergraduate degree or higher with another 18.6% reporting that their mothers did some college coursework. Seventy percent of these students are employed, either full time or part time.

Appendix 2 presents the descriptive statistical results for the various background areas and the "current" semester (i.e., the semester in which they participated in the math quizzes for this study). With respect to economics background, approximately 27.1% of the students tested had already completed one college-level course in economics principles. Over 84% of the students took economics in high school, not surprising since the State of Georgia requires completion of high school economics as a graduation requirement. The remaining 16% who did not take economics in high school primarily come from out of state students, older students, and students who dropped out of high school without completing the economics requirement but have since earned the G.E.D. (General Equivalency Diploma). The average estimated number of economics classes missed in the current semester was 2.6 classes (noting that these descriptive statistics were gathered at the same time that the end of the semester math quiz was administered).

More than 70% of the students report successful completion of a college level math class prior to the current semester. In addition, 34% of the students were in enrolled in a college level math course while taking economics and participating in this study,; likewise, 24% were enrolled in a college level accounting course in the current semester. High school math backgrounds show that, although the vast majority of students completed Algebra 1, Algebra 2 and Geometry, only about half of the students took trigonometry, less than one-fourth studied pre-calculus, and only one eighth enrolled in calculus while in high school.

An examination of college backgrounds reveals that 16% of students had previously attended a four-year college or university and that 16.4% of the students report loss of financial aid due to poor academic performance. In the current semester, approximatelty 65% of the students receive financial aid and 53% report receiving academic scholarships. This seemingly high number is not surprising given the State of Georgia's Hope scholarship program which gives high school students a significant tuition scholarship if they achieved a B average in core high school classes; yet they only retain the scholarship if they maintain a B average in college each year.

5. Empirical Results

The number of participants was almost split evenly between the two faculty members, with 50.4% of the students coming from one professor's classes and 49.6% coming from the other professor's classes. With 258 students total, it was statistically determined that there was no significant difference in the mean difference in math quiz scores between the two faculty members (results not presented). Thus the students were combined as one group for the purpose of this research.

In order to investigate where there is a distinction between the average difference in student quiz performance in the Fall (F) vs. the Spring (S) semester, a two-tailed t-test is utilized to test H_0: $(\mu_2 - \mu_1)_F - (\mu_2 - \mu_1)_S = 0$ vs. H_1: $(\mu_2 - \mu_1)_F - (\mu_2 - \mu_1)_S \neq 0$. The equal variance assumption of the t-test is rejected since the F-statistic is significant at a value of 3.804. On a 12-point scale, the average difference in score for the Fall is 0.81 and the average difference in score for the Spring is 0.86; the resulting value of the test statistic ($t = 0.216$), with 185 degrees of freedom, is clearly not significant. Thus there is no difference in the average of the difference in quiz scores between the Fall and the Spring semesters, and data from both semesters is thus treated as one data set.

To examine whether there is a statistically significant difference in the student quiz scores on the beginning quiz (quiz 1) and the end of the semester quiz (quiz 2), a two-tailed paired sample t-test is used to test H_0: $\mu_2 - \mu_1 = 0$ vs. H_1: $\mu_2 - \mu_1 \neq 0$. On a 12-point scale, the average quiz 1 score is 7.18 and the average quiz 2 score is 8.01, resulting in a difference of the averages of 0.83. With 257 degrees of freedom, the value of the test statistic ($t = 7.307$) is highly significant with a p-value of approximately 0.000. Thus there is a significant difference between the average beginning and ending quiz scores with quiz scores higher at the end of the semester indicating an improvement in basic math skills over the course of the semester.

After determining the presence of a significant difference between quiz results at the beginning and at the end of the semester, we then search for an explanation of this difference. Some of the independent variables collected are clearly control variables and must remain in the model on a priori grounds. For example, the dummy variables indicating the respondent's concurrent enrollment in math or accounting control for influences other than economics that may affect the development of math skills over a semester. We then use a "testing down" procedure, controlling the overall α-value at 5 percent by appropriately adjusting the α levels at each step. The model presented in Table 3 emerges as the most parsimonious representation of the relationship between the difference in math quiz scores and its determinants.

The calculated F-statistic is highly significant indicating that the R-squared is significantly different from zero. As expected, the coefficient on Prior Math was positive and significant showing that successful completion of a collegiate non-remedial math course is correlated with an improvement in math skill. Perhaps taking an economics course helps a student to refresh concepts already familiar from earlier math courses. Prior Econ is significant and negative indicating that

Table 3
Estimated Model

	Coefficient	p-value
Intercept	-0.216	0.874
Prior Econ	-0.539*	0.072
Prior Math	0.883**	0.016
Required	0.003	0.926
Dad's Education	-0.265***	0.007
Age	0.010*	0.081
Gender	-0.468*	0.078
Current Math	0.118	0.707
Current Acct	-0.231	0.310
Instructor	0.361	0.181
GPA	-0.232	0.330
R-squared	0.145	
F-statistic	2.894***	0.002

any benefit to math skills from taking economics may be already realized in the first college level economics course taken by the student.

The coefficient on Gender in the model is significant and negative suggesting that the math skills of male respondents show greater improvement than the math skills of female respondents. This result is consistent with the research finding of Anderson, Benjamin and Fuss (1994) that there is a male grade premium in economics courses and with Benedict and Hoag (2002) who find that females are more apprehensive about both math and economics than males.

Age is a positive significant variable explaining the difference in math skill quiz scores. This result is consistent with the research of Bonello, Swartz, and Davidson (1984) that finds increased experience in the college environment is advantageous to successful performance in economics courses. The variable Dad's Education is a categorical variable measuring the respondent's father's highest level of formal education. The estimated coefficient is highly significant and negative. This does not suggest that a higher level of education of the father is associated with lower math skills but rather with a lowered improvement in skills over the course of a semester. This result may imply that the gains from a higher level of parental education are already realized by the beginning of the student's college economics coursework thus leaving less scope for improvement.

Interestingly, the estimated coefficients on the variables Current Math and Current Accounting are not significantly different from zero. These variables represent the student's enrollment in other courses that may develop math skills during the same semester in which the respondent is participating in the study. Therefore these other courses do not appear to be significant variables explaining the difference in math quiz scores.

As a further investigation of this result, the average difference in student quiz performances is examined for any difference between those students currently enrolled in accounting (A) vs. this not currently enrolled in accounting (NA). A two-tailed t-test is utilized to test H_0: $(\mu_2 - \mu_1)_{NA} - (\mu_2 - \mu_1)_A = 0$ vs. H_1: $(\mu_2 - \mu_1)_{NA} - (\mu_2 - \mu_1)_A \neq 0$. The equal variance assumption of the t-test is not rejected since the F-statistic is insignificant at a value of 0.166. On a 12-point scale, the average difference in score for those students currently enrolled in accounting is 0.87 and for those not currently enrolled in accounting is 0.82. The value of the test statistics ($t = -0.150$), with 256 degrees of freedom, is clearly not significant with a resulting p-value of 0.881. Thus there is no significant difference in the average of the difference in quiz scores between those students currently taking accounting and those not currently taking accounting.

Similarly, the average difference in student quiz performances is investigated for any difference between those students currently taking a mathematics course (M) vs. those not currently taking mathematics (NM). Again, a two-tailed test examines H_0: $(\mu_2 - \mu_1)_{NM} - (\mu_2 - \mu_1)_M = 0$ vs. H_1: $(\mu_2 - \mu_1)_{NM} - (\mu_2 - \mu_1)_M \neq 0$. The equal variance assumption of the t-test is rejected with a calculated F-statistic of 4.570. The average difference in score for those students currently enrolled in mathematics is 0.74 and for those not currently enrolled in mathematics is 0.85. The resulting t-statistic ($t=0.482$) is not significant with a p-value of 0.630 and 249 degrees of freedom. There is no statistically significant difference in the average of the difference in quiz scores between those students currently taking mathematics and those who are not enrolled in mathematics.

The results of these two t-tests confirm the results of the model; these other two courses, accounting and mathematics, although currently taken at the same time as students participated in this study, are not significant explanatory variables behind the improvement in math quiz performance.

6. Conclusion

The results of this large sample-size project indicate that taking a college-level economics course improves student math skills. The quiz content was designed to test skills that are generally encountered in the principles classroom, and current enrollment in accounting and in college level mathematics courses are insignificant to explain improvement in quiz scores. Variables such as age, sex, father's education level, and successful prior completion of a college level math course are all significant. Interestingly, prior exposure to college level economics is also significant but negative, suggesting that any improvement in basic math skills due to principles of economics occurs in the first principles course taken.

This study provides evidence of particular note as math literacy is increasingly recognized as an essential skill, and as the possible inclusion of a mathematics portion to the University System of Georgia's Regents' Testing program is under investigation. Successful completion of this test of basic reading and writing skills during the first two years of college is necessary both for receiving a two-year college transfer degree and for further advancement to higher education in the State of Georgia, and the addition of a math literacy component would be a significant expansion. There is a common perception that, outside of the mathematics classroom, it is only the science curriculum that builds and reinforces student math skills. However, the results of this study demonstrate that economics, a social science, also contributes to the reinforcement of student math skills. The significance of prior completion of a college math course in explaining math quiz score improvement indicates that economics indeed reminds the students of previously encountered mathematical concepts—and reminds educators of the importance of repetition in the learning process.

References and Readings

Anderson, G., D, Benjamin, and M.A. Fuss (1994) "The determinants of success in university introductory economics courses," *Journal of Economic Education* 25: 99-119.

Ballard, C.L. and M.F. Johnson (2004) "Research in economic education—basic math skills and performance in an introductory economics class," *Journal of Economic Education* 35: 3-23.

Becker, W.E. (2000) "Teaching economics in the 21st Century," *Journal of Economic Perspectives* 14: 109-119.

Benedict, M.E. and J. Hoag (2002) "Who's afraid of their economics classes? Why are students apprehensive about introductory economics courses? An empirical investigation," *American Economist* 46: 31-45.

Berry, L. (2003) "Bridging the gap: A community college and area high school collaboration," *Community College Journal of Research and Practice* 27.

Bonello, F.J., T.R. Swartz, and W.I. Davidson (1984) "Freshman-sophomore learning differentials: A comment," *Journal of Economic Education* 15: 205-210.

Buscena, D. and M. Watts (2001) "Do prerequisites matter? Analysis of intermediate microeconomics grades," *Review of Agricultural Economics* 23: 203-213.

Evensky, J. D. Kao, Q. Yang and R. Fadele (1997) "Addressing prerequisite mathematics needs—a case study in introductory economics," *International Journal of Mathematic Education in Science & Technology* 28: 629-636.

Espey, M. (1997) "Testing math competency in introductory economics," *Review of Agricultural Economics* 19: 484-491.

Fizel, J.L. and J.D. Johnson (1986) "The effect of macro/micro course sequencing on learning and attitudes in principles of economics," *Journal of Economic Education* 17: 87-98.

Kennedy, P. (1998) *A guide to econometrics*, Cambridge, MA: The MIT Press.

Kroncke, C. and L. Smyth (2003) "The effectiveness of using electronic slides to teach graphical economic concepts," *Journal of Economics and Finance Education* 2: 38-46.

Milkman, M., J. McCoy and D. Brassfield (1995) "Some additional evidence on the effect of university math on student performance in principles of economics," *Journal of Research and Development in Education* 28: 220-229.

Park, K. and P. Kerr (1990) "Determinants of academic performance: A multinomial logit approach," *Journal of Economic Education* 21: 101-111.

Pindyck, R. and D. Rubinfeld (1981) *Econometric models and economic forecasts*, New York, NY: McGraw-Hill.

Appendix 1
Example of the Math Skills Quiz

1. Suppose you see a shirt in a store that costs $50. You return the next week and find that the shirt has been marked down on sale to $30. What is the percentage saved on the price of the shirt (in other words, what percentage is the sale?)?

    a. 60%   b. 66.67%   c. 33.33%   d. 40%

2. Suppose that z=x/y and you know that z = 5 and x = 15. Find the value of y.

    a. 15   b. 75   c. 3   d. 1/3

3. Perform the following division: (1/6)÷(2/3)

    a. 9   b. 1/4   c. 1/9   d. 4

4. Consider two variables, X and Y. If you observe that X decreases from a value of 13 to 9, and in response, Y increases from a value of 2 to 4, then we say that X and Y have:

    a. a negative relationship
    b. a positive relationship
    c. a neutral relationship
    d. there is not enough information given to determine their relationship

5. Consider the graph below.

    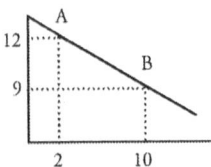

    The coordinates of point A are (2,12) and the coordinates of point B are (10,9). Find the slope of the line.

    a. 3/8   b. -3/8   c. 8/3   d. -8/3

6. Suppose the value of X is 6. Find the absolute value of X.

    a. -6   b. 6   c. 1/6   d. not enough information given to answer

7. Suppose you want to carpet a room that is 12 feet long and 8 feet wide. The carpet you've chosen costs $2 per square foot. How much will it cost to purchase enough carpet?

    a. $96   b. $192   c. $40   d. $48

8. Consider the graph below:

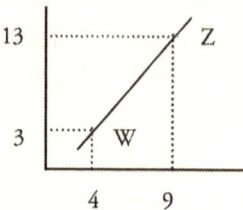

The coordinates of point W are (4,3) and the coordinates of point Z are (9,13). Find the slope of the line.

a. ½   b. -2   c. 10   d. 2

9. Suppose the value of Y is -8. Find the absolute value of Y.

a. 1/8   b. -8   c. 8   d. not enough information given to answer

10. Which of the graphs below show a point of tangency between lines A and B?

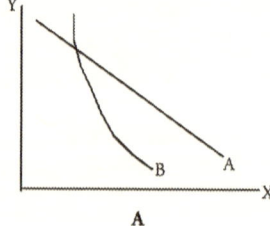

A

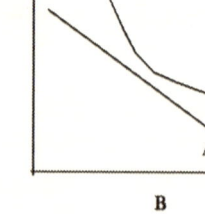

B

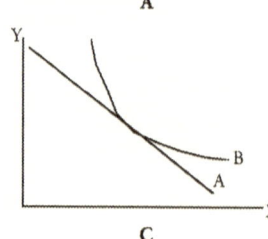

C

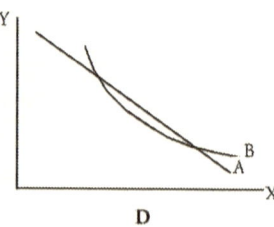

D

11. Suppose a bakery receives an order for three containers of their very special cookies. Each container will have 20 cookies in it, and the total cost of producing enough cookies to fill a single container is $40. What is the bakery's average production cost per cookie?

a. $0.50   b. $6   c. $0.67   d. $2

12. Solve the following equation for Q: Q = 48 + (1/4)Q

a. 64   b. 36   c. 16   d. 12

Appendix 2
Descriptive Statistics

		% yes
Econ Background	PriorEcon (prior successful completion of a college level economics class)	27.1%
	High School Economics class	83.6
	Required (economics required for major)	61.2
Math Background	PriorMath (prior successful completion of a college level math class)	71.0
	High School Algebra 1	91.2
	High School Algebra 2	87.6
	High School Geometry	92.4
	High School Trigonometry	49.6
	High School Pre-Calculus	23.5
	High School Calculus	12.2
College Background	Prior attendance at a four-year college or university	15.7
	Prior attendance at any college	20.0
	Prior loss of financial aid due to poor grades	16.4
Current Semester Information	Current Math (current enrollment in a college level math course)	34.0
	Current Acct (current enrollment in a principles of accounting course)	24.0
	Current recipient of financial aid	65.2
	Low interest student loans	16.5
	Veterans' benefits	3.4
	Academic scholarship (including State of Georgia Hope Scholarship)	53.4
	Athletic scholarship	5.3
	Other aid	20.4
Other variables		Average
	Cumulative GPA (on a 4.0 scale)	3.00
	Estimated # of economics classes missed by student in the semester	2.60
	Current # of semester hours coursework	13.16
	Estimated current # of hrs spent in extracurricular activities per week	1.35

4

Synchronous and Asynchronous Delivery in MBA Instruction
An Empirical Examination of the Differences in Student Performance*

WILLIAM S. SCHANINGER, JR., ROBERT E. NIEBUHR, AND DANIEL M. GROPPER

I. Introduction

In 1997, Peter Drucker offered the following observation regarding higher education in the United States (Lenzner, 1997: 126):

> "Thirty years from now the big university campuses will be relics. Universities won't survive. It's as large a change as when we got the printed book...Higher education is in deep crisis...Already we are beginning to deliver more lectures...via satellite or two-way video at a fraction of the cost. The college won't survive as a residential institution."

What was the change that Drucker was referring to? What could possibly be occurring on campuses nationwide that would engender a comparison with the impact of the printed word? What could elicit such an apocalyptic prophesy from a modern day business legend? The mainstream implementation of distance education is the change that Drucker was addressing.

With facilitating technology improving on a daily basis, universities are seeking out opportunities to service parts of the population previously inaccessible to them (Blumenstyk, 1999b). While many schools have just begun to explore these opportunities, others have arisen as exclusively distance education based institutions. Universities such as the University of Maryland, Queen's University, the University of Pennsylvania, Johns Hopkins University, and Duke University have embraced the distance learning approach (Potashnik and Capper, 1998; Webster and Hackley, 1997).

The rapid emergence of accredited schools in the distance learning environment has given this approach to higher education greater legitimacy. In 1995, 33% of all higher education institutions offered some form of distance education (Kirk and Bartelstein, 1999). In 1997, 1,000 institutions of higher learning offered distance education courses (Lozado, 1997). In 1998, 85% reported to be currently offering or planning to offer distance education courses (National Center, 1998). In a 1999 AACSB study, it was determined that almost 40% of the responding colleges of business were already offering distance learning degree programs (AACSB, 1999). Harris (1999) claims that in the next decade, it is expected that the demand for distance based higher education will increase by at least 30%. Interestingly, for individuals to remain fully employed in the economy, they need post-secondary education or training (Harris, 1999).

One answer to the anticipated increase in demand is to form publicly funded "virtual" universities. These universities are formed through consortiums of existing traditional universities to provide all of their courses in a distance format through the "virtual" entity. One example of this in the United States is the Western Governors' University. Additionally, federal funds have been specifically set aside by the Department of Education to explore and evaluate the content, quality, and viability of distance education programs (The Institute, 1999). It would appear that distance education is not only here to stay, but it is becoming a more visible option in the menu of higher education offerings. Given this standing, the exploration of this burgeoning niche appears appropriate.

The purpose of this paper is four fold: 1) To identify a common definition of distance education; 2) To empirically explore the impact that asynchronous delivery of educational material has on student outcomes; 3) To explore if women experience outcomes similar to men in the distance education classes; and 4) To determine if relevant demographic variables are capable of predicting student outcomes in a distance-learning environment.

2. Defining Distance Education

Distance education has been labeled a variety of things: distance learning, correspondence courses, asynchronous transfer medium, computer mediated learning, etc. However, the definition of the concept of distance education has remained relatively stable over time. Clark and Verduin (1989) attributed the 1960s conceptualization to Otto Peters who popularized distance education in Europe. His definition asserts that distance education is formal study where the instructor and student are separated during the delivery of the material. Holmberg (1985; as cited in Bartlett and Holley, 1996) identified distance education as "various forms of study at all levels which are not under the continuous, immediate supervision of a tutor...nevertheless, benefit from the planning, guidance, and tuition of a tutorial organization (p. 2)". Guerrero and Kelly (1998: 31) established three themes from the definitions of distance education they found; "(1) learning involves a geographical distance between the instructor and learner, (2) opportunity for face to face interactive communication between the instructor and learner is more limited than in the traditional classroom, and (3) some type of medium is involved to span the geographical distance between the teacher and the learner." Hickman (1999) embraces brevity when describing distance education as an organized learning activity that occurs away from the setting where it (the learning) is usually conducted. Finally, Davey (1999) suggests that distance education is occurring any time that the instructor and student are separated by time or distance. Given those definitions, the following is offered:

> *Distance education is a form of knowledge transfer that occurs without regard to temporal or proximal synchronicity. The instructor/provider is able to deliver content in an asynchronous fashion that facilitates the convenient accessing of the material by the student/customer. The ingredient that facilitates these transfers is a technological medium (tv, radio, two-way video, videotape, internet, etc.) that is appropriate for the depth and breadth of the content delivered.*

The literature that exists on distance education is largely anecdotal and opinion based with relatively little empirical work (Merisotis and Phipps, 1999). The empirical work that does exist is largely positive towards distance education (for a lengthy discussion of the relative merits of this work see Merisotis and Phipps, 1999). However, there remains a significant stream of literature that is critical of distance-based, higher education. In response to this schism, both positive and negative opinions will be reviewed before establishing research questions.

3. Opinions on Distance Learning: A Review of Recent Literature

One of the most salient reasons for why distance education is attractive to educational institution administrators is economies of scale. Distance education programs can use existing resources to expand the universities' ability to serve a much wider audience within the populace (Hickman, 1999). The opportunity to provide education to under-served portions of the population is often both an institutional and public policy issue. By implementing a distance education program, both issues can be addressed. The use of these technologies provides the university with the tools to simultaneously reach large numbers of students without significant capital investment (Guerrero and Miller, 1998). Further, administrators can view the initiation of a distance education as a win-win opportunity for them. By starting the program, the institution will serve portions of the market not previously addressed by the traditional on-campus programs. In addition, the program will force students to become comfortable with technologies (email, video, etc.) that are necessary for success in the modern business environment (Webster and Hackley, 1997).

One might ask what the benefit of higher education is. Farber (1998) reports that college educated people tend to be more flexible, open to new ideas, tolerant of ambiguity, more socially adjusted than the norm, and comfortable discussing abstract concepts. In addition, these people were found to be more oriented towards rational decision making patterns, willing to get involved in politics, appreciative of the arts, and internally motivated regarding work. While these are all wonderful attributes, can we reasonably expect the same from individuals who get the educational experience in a non-residential manner?

Thomas Russell (1997) would suggest yes. He maintains a web site that details the findings of 355 papers, manuscripts, and projects that concluded there is no "significant" difference in student outcomes between traditional students and distance education students. The majority of these papers are opinion or anecdotal pieces. While there are some significant methodological issues with many of the empirical papers (e.g., the Wang and Newlin (2000) study of web instruction versus classroom instruction did not control for individual differences), Russell's extensive compilation of studies makes a compelling argument for the finding of no adverse impact on student performance from distance learning approaches.

As stated earlier, there are some very ardent opponents to the expansion of distance education. It would be very easy to dismiss criticisms out of hand by claiming that professional academics (from whom the majority of the criticisms originate) are instilled with a sense of preservation that pervades all thinking on this issue. However, to do so would be to ignore an opportunity to honestly assess distance education programs with a critical eye. Thus, the criticisms about to be presented are intended to open a dialog about this issue rather than condemn such programs out of hand.

The majority of criticism is derived from anecdotal or opinion pieces that tend to focus on the credibility of distance education (Potashnik and Capper, 1998) and on the issue of instructor-student interaction. Many scholars still believe that a distance-based program is inferior (Clark and Verduin, 1989; Walling, 1996). By our definition, we describe distance learning as something that is not bound by proximal or temporal synchronicity. Thus, the instructor and student have very little "live," one on one interaction. Some academics assess distance learning as merely receiving knowledge because it is, ostensibly, without the interaction and support of the faculty (Blumenstyk, 1997). Certainly one of the drawbacks to any of the asynchronous delivery mechanisms is a lack of personal interaction with the instructor and cohort group (Guerrero and Miller, 1998). While the technology available can leverage the instructor's time and make him/her more productive, it cannot replace time spent with students (Merisotis and Phipps, 1999). In addition, there are other complaints about distance learning programs. One is that the student may feel isolated because they do not have steady contact with a cohort group. The other is that in research based distance education programs, the ability to gain access to a library is critical and is not often available to distance graduate students (Kirk and Bartelstein, 1999).

It has been purported that women do not do as well in distance education programs because they do not like the distance setting. Specifically, women have been assigned the label of not liking to communicate through email, of not liking to express opinion in group settings, and needing an extremely collegial atmosphere (Koch, 1998; Blumenstyk, 1997). Apparently, those issues did not arise in our sample or if they did, it was not to a point where it influenced performance. In addition, empirical literature that has looked expressly at women has found cases where the woman performed at or above their male companions (Blumenstyk, 1997).

While there are mixed opinions on the subject of distance-learning, this paper will focus specifically on outcomes, i.e., the performance of students in a distance-learning environment contrasted with the performance of students in a traditional campus approach. The following research questions will be address:

R1—Do distance education students perform as well as on-campus students?

R2—Do women perform at a disproportionately lower level in the distance education setting?

R3—Do the demographic variables of age, GMAT score, undergraduate GPA, undergraduate major, undergraduate school, etc. contribute to predicting student performance?

These questions are addressed empirically below.

4. The Empirical Model

Demographic data for this project were collected from the admission records of 296 graduate business (MBA) students enrolled in a large university in the southeastern United States. For this sample, 67 percent were male and 33 percent female. Fifty-two percent of the students were traditional, on-campus students while 48% were in a distance-based program. The distance-based program had been in existence for over five years and consisted primarily of providing the same course lectures via videotape to the distance students. These distance students received the same text, cases, handouts, and other materials as the campus

Table 1
Means, Standard Deviations and Correlations

Variable	Mean	S. Dev.	1	2	3	4	5	6
1 Gender	0.3277	0.4702	1					
2 Age	27.325	5.8623	-0.17	1				
3 GMAT	553.46	75.574	-0.28	0.053	1			
4 Undergrad. GPA	3.1281	0.3833	0.167	-0.003	-0.017	1		
5 Undergrad. Major	1.0272	1.0512	0.093	-0.022	-0.18	0.01	1	
6 Work Years.	4.585	5.5528	-0.144	0.892	0.078	-0.024	-0.014	1
7 Video./Campus	0.5169	0.5006	0.171	-0.437	-0.167	0.019	0.123	-0.45
8 GMAT-Q%	57.436	23.924	-0.29	-0.009	0.84	-0.074	-0.238	0.016
9 GMAT-V%	64.465	20.267	-0.091	0.054	0.726	0.046	0.049	0.074
10 GMAT-Total %	64.280	21.483	-0.246	0.022	0.96	-0.046	-0.142	0.048
11 Ugrad. School	2.914	1.9489	-0.055	0.126	-0.111	0.142	0.147	0.11
12 Quarter	4.0608	2.1096	0.048	0.075	0.129	0.014	-0.247	0.066
13 Case Course Gr.	2.63e-15	1	0.118	0.148	-0.028	0.171	-0.134	0.126
14 Essay Course Gr.	1.57e-15	1	0042	0.143	0.218	0.364	0.142	0.143
15 Quant Cou. Gr.	8.13e-16	1	0.074	-0.02	0.263	0.107	-0.231	0.025

	7	8	9	10	11	12	13	14	15
7 Video/Campus	1								
8 GMAT-Q%	-0.124	1							
9 GMAT-V%	-0.079	0.331	1						
10 GMAT-Total %	-0.14	0.826	0.729	1					
11 Ugrad. School	-0.102	-0.106	-0.045	-0.121	1				
12 Quarter	-0.403	0.154	0.022	0.114	-0.008	1			
13 Case Course Grade	-0.232	-0.006	-0.134	-0.018	0.177	0.030	1		
14 Essay Course Grade	-0.094	0.291	0.081	0.232	-0.003			1	
15 Quant Course Grade	0.064	0.274	0.095	0.226	-0.222	0.321			1

students and took the same tests with identical instructions and time limits. In this study, we examined groups of students from three different types of course testing designs, the faculty being the same for both the campus and distance deliveries of the three courses. Faculty were available by telephone or email if the distance-based students had questions on course content or other matters. The students' age ranged from 21 to 56 with a mean of 27. GMAT scores ranged from 400 to 760 with a mean score of 553. A more detailed exploration of the demographic breakdown of this sample is provided in Tables 1 and 2. Descriptive statistics and intercorrelations were calculated for all variables utilized and are presented in Table 1. Table 2 indicates that the distance MBA differed from the campus MBA students in several aspects. They were older and had more work experience and also had a higher average GMAT score.

Table 2
Group Means for Comparison of Campus and Distance-Based Students

Variable	Total	Campus	Distance	F
Age	27.7 [338]	25.0 [161]	30.2 [177]	77.1*
GMAT	555 [336]	540 [163]	569 [173]	13.2*
Undergraduate GPA	3.14 [331]	3.15 [158]	3.12 [173]	0.5
Years of Work Exp.	4.7 [342]	2.2 [168]	7.2 [174]	83.5*
Case-based course grade	84.4 [183]	82.3 [96]	86.7 [87]	11.2*
Essay-based course grade	90.8 [88]	90.5 [49]	91.1 [39]	0.5
Quantitative course grade	86.6 [126]	87.3 [62]	86.0 [64]	0.5

Notes: The numbers in brackets below the means are observations for each category. * denotes $p<0.001$.

The data utilized in this study were collected from one quarter to four years after the students had taken the courses. Grade data were collected only when the instructor taught the course to the distance-based students and the on-campus students at the same time. MBA program admission files were accessed to provide demographic data for each student. Once the grade was matched to the demographic data, any identifying features of the data were removed.

Independent Variables

Gender:	This variable is coded as a binary (dummy) variable. A value of 0 indicates a male respondent and 1 indicates a female respondent. This is a demographic control variable.
Age:	This continuous variable denotes the age of the respondent at the time they applied to the program. This is another demographic control variable.
Work Years:	This continuous variable describes the number of years of work experience the student has had at the time of their admission to the MBA program.
GMAT:	The Graduate Management Admissions Test (GMAT) is the verbal and quantitative reasoning/skills test required for admission to the MBA program. It is a proxy for general cognitive ability or "G." This continuous variable will range between 200 and 800.
GMAT-V%:	This is the percentile ranking for the student's verbal portion of the GMAT. This is used to control for any variation in the actual GMAT test over time.
GMAT-Q%:	This is the percentile ranking for the student's quantitative portion of the GMAT. This is used to control for any variation in the actual GMAT test over time.
GMAT-T%:	This is the percentile ranking for the student's overall score on the GMAT. This is used to control for any variation in the actual GMAT test over time.
Underg. GPA:	This is the undergraduate grade point average. The values here will range from 0 to 4.0. This was also utilized as a control variable related to academic ability.
Underg. Major:	This variable is a categorical variable intended to address the type of undergraduate major the respondent had. The variable is coded in an ordinal fashion (0=engineering, 1=math/science, 3=liberal arts, and 4=other). An ordinal approach to coding was chosen for this data in an effort to

depict a perceived relationship between undergraduate major and quantitative orientation. This variable was created under the assumption that engineering students were in general, more quantitatively oriented. This is consistent with other researchers attempting to model student performance while controlling for individual student differences (Caudill and Gropper, 1991).

Distance/Campus: This variable is categorical. In this case, 1 denotes that the student received the course in a distance learning/asynchronous format (one-way video) and 0 denotes that the student received instruction in a synchronous format (on-campus lecture).

Criterion Variables

The use of grades as a criterion is well established in this literature stream (Burton, 1998; National Center, 1998). Hickman (1999) reported that determining quality in distance education programs was generally accomplished by measuring grades. The use of course grades is supported by Farber (1998) who acknowledges that measurable competence (as represented by grades) often represents the core of the course. While the grade alone does not capture the richness of student achievement in its entirety, it is a more valid measure of student outcomes than anecdotal comments provided in many previous studies. For each of the following three types of course testing designs the campus and distance students had the same instructor, same course content, and the same course grading criteria. The difference between the instructional pedagogy is that the campus students experienced synchronous content delivery versus the distance students receiving asynchronous content delivery.

Case-Based Course Test Average: This course is primarily focused on analyzing and applying the principles of organizational change to a variety of case-based scenarios. It has little to no quantitative expectations. The outcome variable here is test average. This variable has been standardized to address issues regarding grade inflation and range restriction.

Essay-Based Course Test Average: This course is primarily focused on the principles of micro and macro economic theory. It encompasses both a conceptual and quantitative component. The outcome variable used here is the course test average from a series of essay question tests. This variable has been standardized to address issues regarding grade inflation and range restriction.

Quantitative Course Test Average: This course is focused primarily on the fundamental of statistical analysis and its application in an operations setting. There is virtually no conceptual component to this course; it is almost exclusively driven by quantitative expectations. The outcome variable for this course is test average. This variable has been standardized to address issues regarding grade inflation and range restriction.

Methodological Concerns

In "What's the Difference?", Merisotis and Phipps (1999) review the current (1990s) empirical literature that has examined the outcomes of distance education programs. The authors were able to clearly identify several shortcomings in the research. This paper's research design is intended to address most of the issues brought out in the Merisotis and Phipps report.

Controlling for extraneous variables was identified as the primary shortcoming in the existing literature. For this study we have included ten demographic variables to address the issue. Clearly, if variance is being accounted for by individual differences, that point must be addressed prior to making attributions about the relative merits (or lack thereof) of distance education.

Not randomly assigning subjects was identified as a shortcoming in the existing literature. The data for this study were taken from classes that received exactly the same pedagogy and course expectations. The courses included in this study were always taught and taped on campus for distribution to the distance-based students. While not randomly assigned, the assumption here is that with appropriate controlling for extraneous variables and by insuring that the delivery mechanism was the same, this study can avoid the confounds identified in the Merisotis and Phipps (1999) work.

Not controlling for reactive effects was also identified as a shortcoming in the existing literature. Specifically, "Novelty Effect" and "John Henry Effect" were mentioned. It is important to note that data collection occurred well after the grade sheets were turned in by the instructors. Thus, there was no experiment for which the students would change their behavior since they were unaware of any research that might be done.

Analysis

Hierarchical regression was utilized as the primary analysis procedure. Criterion variables were predicted individually. All demographic variables were loaded in the initial block, with the predictor of interest being loaded last and in a separate block to establish an overall R^2 for the model as well as an incremental R^2 for the predictor of interest. In the case of Research Question 2, the use of an interaction term appeared appropriate and one was calculated for use in the regression equation. In this analysis, the interaction term was added in as the last predictor. It was regressed against the three criterions individually. In addition, the beta weights (in the full models) for each demographic variable provided the information necessary to answer that research question. It should be noted that several of the variables collected were not utilized in the final regression models due to problems with multicollinearity.

5. Empirical Results

Research Question 1: Do distance education students perform as well as on-campus students?

Without any consideration for control variables, Table 2 did indicate that the distance students achieved a higher average grade in the case-based course. Table 3 presents the results from the hierarchical regression analysis for the three criterion variables. It appears that in this sample, after accounting for demographic variables, distance education students fair as well as traditional students regardless of the course content. For the case-based course grade the full model was non-significant (F=1.213; p=.298) and the distance education (distance/campus) variable was not significant. For the essay-based course the overall model was

Table 3
Multiple Hierarchical Regressions

Variable	Case-Based Course β	Sig.	Essay-Based Course β	Sig.	Quantitative Course β	Sig.
(Constant)		0.434		0.000		0.007
Gender	0.123	0.280	0.117	0.373	0.182	0.069
Undergrad GPA	0.131	0.243	0.334	0.006	0.125	0.188
Undergrad Major	-0.044	0.718	0.115	0.373	-0.212	0.032
Work Years	0.011	0.934	0.133	0.307	0.145	0.171
GMAT-Q%	0.042	0.735	0.254	0.074	0.263	0.017
GMAT-V%	-0.101	0.398	0.078	0.528	0.046	0.657
Undergrad School	0.134	0.222	-0.017	0.888	-0.123	0.208
Quarter	0.009	0.936			0.274	0.005
Distance/Campus	-0.204	0.139	0.006	0.970	0.148	0.166
F	1.23		2.703		3.719	
R^2	0.113		0.268		0.283	
Sig	0.298		0.013		0.001	

significant (F=2.703; p=.013) but the distance/campus variable was not significant. Finally, with regard to the quantitative course, the overall model is significant (F=3.719; p=.001) but the distance/campus variable was not significant. These results are consistent with numerous other studies (Koch, 1998; Russell, 1998; Walling, 1996; Clark and Verduin, 1996). In all of those pieces, the distance learners were found to have done as well or exceeded the traditional learners.

Research Question 2: Do women perform at a disproportionately lower level in the distance education setting?

No, they do not. The interaction term between gender and distance education variable was insignificant for each criterion. Table 4 presents the results of the hierarchical regression models that utilized interaction terms to explore this question for all three criterion variables. With respect to the case-based class the interaction term was not significant (p=.58). For the essay-based class the interaction term also produced non-significant results (p=.323). Finally, in the quantitative

Table 4
Multiple Hierarchical Regression Testing for Interaction Effect

Variable	Case-Based Course		Essay-Based Course		Quantitative Course	
	β	Sig.	β	Sig.	β	Sig.
(Constant)		0.285		0.000		0.019
Undergrad GPA	0.149	0.178	0.350	0.003	0.135	0.161
Undergrad Major	-0.096	0.422	0.139	0.277	-0.181	0.069
Work Years	0.106	0.357	0.158	0.188	0.083	0.415
GMAT-Q%	0.058	0.643	0.253	0.070	0.221	0.044
GMAT-V%	-0.158	0.176	0.087	0.474	0.039	0.711
Undergrad School	0.152	0.169	-0.022	0.847	-0.158	0.113
Quarter	0.052	0.639			0.276	0.006
Gender×Distance	0.065	0.567	0.122	0.348	0.071	0.494
F		1.024	F	3.141	F	3.421
R^2		0.086	R^2	0.268	R^2	0.241
Sig		0.425	Sig	0.007	Sig	0.002

class, the interaction term was also insignificant (p=.706). Apparently, the issues concerning negative female reaction to distance learning did not arise in our sample, or if they did, it was not to a point where it influenced performance.

Research Question 3: Do the demographic variables of Years of Work Experience, GMAT score, Undergraduate GPA, Undergraduate Major, Undergraduate School, etc. contribute to predicting student outcomes?

As indicated in Table 3, there was limited support for the impact of demographic variables as a predictor of outcomes. Only four of a potential 18 relationships were significant. For instance, undergraduate GPA was a significant predictor for the essay-based class (p=0.006), while it remained insignificant for the case-based and quantitative courses (p=.243 and p=.188, respectively). Similarly, undergraduate major was a significant predictor for the quantitative course (p=0.032) but not for the case-based and essay-based courses (p=.718 and p=.373, respectively). Finally, GMAT-Q% was a useful predictor for the quantitative course (p=.074), and not significant for the case-based course (p=.735). While not confirmed in this sample, age has been found to be a positive predictor of success in distance learning programs (Neal, 1999).

6. Discussion and Concluding Comments

Limitations of the Present Study

Some methodological issues will limit the generalizability of these findings. Most importantly, we have limited criterion variables. While measuring competencies with testing devices is more than adequate, it is not ideal. Certainly one of the larger limitations to this approach is the implicitly finite nature of the exam. The exam will never capture completely what is expected of the student and the rest of the course becomes marginalized as it does not lead to a "grade" for the student's effort (Farber, 1998). Additionally, the courses contained in this study were exclusively business school oriented. This same study conducted on a much larger level, across a variety of colleges and content domains would provide far richer evidence for the conclusions drawn here.

Another issue to explore is the absence of any attitudinal measures. It would have been useful to see if the attitudes towards the learning environment would have predicted student outcomes. And similar to this study, would attitudes about the whole distance education process be predictive of student outcomes? Finally, would students' attitudes regarding faculty competence be predictive of student outcomes?

It would have been useful to randomly assign students to sections to thoroughly address potential confounds to external validity. It will continue to be valuable to critically examine research that finds "no significant difference" between those taking distance-education classes and those taking coursework in the traditional sense (Merisotis and Phipps, 1999).

Implications for Practice

While there is expected to be another spike in traditional age students in the coming years, this does not mean that distance learning is going away. Rather, it should serve as a bell-weather that universities will be more likely to take the plunge (or expand existing operations) into a distance-learning program rather than spend precious capital assets on new buildings for students. The trend is already occurring where traditional age students are opting to mix campus-based classes with online/distance courses (AACSB, 1999; Kirk and Bartelstein, 1999).

> "Hickman (1999) highlights the mandate facing distance education: it has to become an integrated mission in public institutions to service all interested segments of the population...adequate partnerships established to provide diversity of resources to the public (p. 19)."

This idea of "access for everyone" is resonating throughout the literature on distance education (Merisotis and Phipps, 1999). Where distance education programs were once the poor stepchild of the higher education family, they are now taking their place at the table with the other more established offerings. In order to foster distance education programs, they must be accorded the same prestige and dignity given to the traditional institutions (Neal, 1999). They must also be provided the support staff necessary to handle the crises as they arise (Potashnik and Capper, 1998).

It is important for educators to understand that not all potential students make good distance-education students. The distance program will require more self-confidence, more self-direction, and more self-efficacy than any other points. Students must be self-motivated (Lozada, 1997) and willing to learn the technology platform that serves as the backbone to service delivery. In this sample, we found that being a distance education student did not significantly impact student performance. Several other variables (e.g., Undergraduate GPA, Undergraduate Major, GMAT-Q%, etc.) did make a difference. The lack of an influence of years of work experience does support studies (e.g., Dreher and Ryan, 2000) that find that previous work experience may have only a small impact on student performance and only in the initial period of a student's program of study. Because there was a difference between courses as to what demographic variables were significant it is appropriate to assume that a "one size fits all" approach to selecting students is probably not appropriate. It does appear that the asynchronous distance education approach is not an inhibitor to success in graduate business programs.

Finally, administrators should be seeing a strong shift away from the mortar and brick paradigm. Repeatedly constructing more buildings is no longer an option for resource constrained institutions who also happen to want to continue serving more people. The fundamental paradigm shift is to viewing distance education as an equal partner in the delivery of higher education service to a variety of constituencies (Dubois, 1996).

* This is a revised version of a paper appearing in the February 2005 issue of the *Journal of Business and Economics Research.*

References

AACSB (1999) "Fifteenth Annual AACSB/UCLA Computer Usage Survey, *Newsline* (Winter), at aacsb.edu/Publications/Newsline.

Barket, R. and C. Holley (1996) "Interactive distance learning: Perspectives and thoughts," *Business Communication Quarterly* 59: 88-97.

Blumenstyk, G. (1997) "A feminist scholar questions how women fare in distance education," *The Chronicle of Higher Education* 44.10: A36.

Blumenstyk, G. (1999a) "In a first, the North Central Association accredits an on-line university," *The Chronicle of Higher Education* 45.28: A27.

Blumenstyk, G. (1999b) "The marketing intensifies in distance learning," *The Chronicle of Higher Education* 45.31: A31.

Burton, R., Jr. (1998) "Costs and benefits of increasing access to a traditional agricultural economics course," *American Journal of Agricultural Economics* 80: 979-984.

Clark, T. and J. Verduin (1989) "Lifelong learning: An omnibus of practice and research," *View* 12: 24-26.

Caudill, S. and D. Gropper (1991) "Test structure, human capital, and student performance on economics exams," *Journal of Economic Education* 22: 303-306.

Davey, K. (1999) "Distance learning demystified," *National Forum* 79: 44-46.

Dreher, G. and K. Ryan (2000) "Prior work experience and academic achievement among first-year MBA students," *Research in Higher Education* 41: 505-525.

Dubois, J. (1996) "Going the distance: A national distance learning initiative," *Adult Learning* 8: 19-21.

Farber, J. (1998) "The third circle: On education and distance learning," *Sociological Perspectives* 41: 797.

Guerrero, L. and T. Miller (1998) "Associations between nonverbal behaviors and initial impressions of instructor competence and course content in videotaped distance education courses," *Communication Education* 47: 30-42.

Harris, D. (1999) "Online education in the United States," *IEEE Communications Magazine* 37.3: 87-93.

Hawkes, M. (1996) "Criteria for evaluating school-based distance education programs," *NASSP Bulletin* 80: 45-52.

Hickman, C. (1999) "Public policy: Implications associated with technology assisted distance learning," *Adult Learning* (Spring): 17-21.

Holmberg, B. (1985) "On the status of distance education in the world in the 1980's: A preliminary report on the fernuniverstitat comparative study," *Zentrales Inst. Fur Fernstudienforschung Arbeitsberich*, 1-34.

The Institute for Higher Education Policy (1999) *Distance Learning in Higher Education*.

Kirk, E. and A. Bartelstein (1999) "Libraries close in on distance education," *Library Journal* 124: 40.

Koch, J. (1998) "How women actually perform in distance education," *The Chronicle of Higher Education* 45.3: A60.

Lenzner, R. (1997) "Seeing things as they really are," *Forbes* 59 (March 10): 122-128.

Lozada, M. (1997) "Look out for distance learning," *Techniques* 72: 24-26.

Merisotis, J. and R. Phipps (1999) "What's the difference?" *Change* 31: 12-17.

National Center for Education Statistics (1998) *Distance Education in Higher Education Institutions: Incidence, Audiences, and Plans to Expand.*

Potashnik, M. and J. Capper (1998) "Distance education: Growth and diversity," *Finance and Development* 35: 42-45.

Russell, T. (1998) "The 'no significant difference' phenomenon," cuda.teleeducation.nb.ca/nosignificantdifference/.

Walling, L. (1996) "Going the distance: Equal education, off campus or on," *Library Journal* 121: 59-62.

Wang, A. and M. Newlin (2000) "Characteristics of students who enroll and succeed in psychology web-based classes," *Journal of Education Psychology* 92: 137-143.

Webster, J. and P. Hackley (1997) "Teaching effectiveness in technology-mediated distance learning," *Academy of Management Journal* 40: 1,282-1,307.

5

Have You Seen the New Econ Prof?
Beauty, Teaching, and Occupational Choice in Higher Education

TRELLIS G. GREEN, FRANKLIN G. MIXON, JR.,
AND LEN J. TREVIÑO

I. Introduction

An expansive literature in social psychology has examined the impact of human beauty on numerous non-economic phenomena (Hamermesh and Parker, 2003). Economists have recently joined this stream of work by examining how beauty shapes economic outcomes, such as a firm's revenues or an individual's labor market earnings (Hamermesh and Biddle, 1994; Biddle and Hamermesh, 1998; Pfann, Biddle, Hamermesh, and Bosman, 2000). The impact of beauty on revenues/earnings is implicitly the end result of the effect of beauty on productivity (Hamermesh and Parker, 2003) or customer discrimination.

A recent trend in empirical research has shown that student evaluations of college instructors are positively related to perceptions of beauty/attractiveness (Boex, 2000; Felton, Mitchell, and Stinson, 2004; Smith, 2005; Hamermesh and Parker, 2003). These results are striking, especially given research indicating that academic administrators employ teaching quality indicators in setting salaries (see Becker and Watts, 1989) and in generating increases in salaries (see Katz, 1973; Siegfried and White, 1973; Kaun, 1984; Moore, Newman and Turnbull, 1998).

This note extends extant literature on the impact of attractiveness on teaching evaluations by examining the role that attractiveness, or physical beauty, plays in professors' occupational choices. In particular, we empirically investigate whether good looking instructors are more (less) likely than their less attractive colleagues to retain academic employment at liberal arts (comprehensive research) colleges/universities, where teaching (research) is the primary focus by which academic administrators determine salaries. To do so, we use a large sample of teacher evaluations from Smith (2005), taken originally from a well-known Internet site designed to support evaluations of university instructors across the United States.

2. Framing the Hypotheses

As a foundation to our aforementioned empirical model, equation (1) adapts the standard wage model of beauty (see Hamermesh and Biddle, 1994; Biddle and Hamermesh, 1998; Hamermesh, Meng, and Zhang, 2002) to higher education:

(1) $W_{ij} = a_j X_i + b_j \theta_i + c_j Z_i + \varepsilon_i$.

W_{ij} is the wage of professor i teaching at university j. *Ceteris paribus*, wage rates reflect marginal productivity, and professors are assumed to choose that university (occupational) setting offering the highest full wage. Each professor is endowed with a vector of standard productivity-enhancing characteristics (X_i) related to teaching, research, and service. Professors are also perceived by their students and others as being attractive (i.e. $\theta_i > 0$), unattractive (i.e., $\theta_i < 0$), or neither (i.e., $\theta_i = 0$).[1] Professors' wages may be affected by these perceptions through the teaching evaluation process. Lastly, a professor's institutional setting (Z_i) is likely to be an integral part of wage determination, given that market incentives influence occupational choice.

We may partition a professor's productivity matrix (X_i) into $(X_T \mid X_R \mid X_S)$ for teaching, research and service activities, respectively, as shown below in (2):

(2) $X_T = \theta[Q_T(\theta_T)] \Rightarrow \theta_T > 0 \quad X_R = \theta[Q_R(\theta_R)] \Rightarrow \theta_R = 0 \quad X_S = \theta[Q_S(\theta_S)] \Rightarrow \theta_S = ?$

In practice, productivity measurement in these diverse academic areas can be proxied with indices of performance quality (e.g., Q_T, Q_R, and Q_S).[2] Recent empirical work has shown that attractiveness is positively (and significantly) related to a professor's teaching performance (i.e., the so-called "fox effect," where $\theta_T > 0$), as measured by student evaluations (Boex, 2000; Felton, Mitchell and Stinson, 2004; Smith, 2005; Hamermesh and Parker, 2003).[3]

Of interest in this study is the effect of perceived attractiveness on the occupational choice of professor i. Therefore, we focus on the X_T component of the academic productivity matrix from (2), where Q_T represents information/characteristics from a formal student teaching evaluation instrument. Information from this instrument is used to proxy performance with quality-enhancing factors such as teaching clarity and rigor.[4] Variable θ_T is an indicator of perceived attractiveness on the part of students. One would expect a sorting or self-selection process to occur in academic labor markets, in which attractive professors would select colleges/universities where the return to attractiveness is maximized, *ceteris paribus*. That return is likely to be greatest at universities/colleges that emphasize teaching over other activities, such as research. Universities (Z), therefore, are classified as either liberal arts ($Z=1$), where teaching is the primary focus, or comprehensive/research ($Z=0$), where i's research endeavors usually exceed his/her teaching performance as the primary focus for reward by academic administrators.[5] Thus, the empirical occupational choice model is given in equation (3) as the probability that professor i is employed by a liberal arts college:

(3) $Prob(Z=1) = [e^I/(1+e^I)]$, where $I = \beta_0 + \beta_1 Q_{Ti} + \beta_2 \theta_{Ti}$.

As equation (3) indicates, professor i's institutional setting is explained by the standard vector Q_{Ti} of teaching quality variables and a measure of perceived attractiveness/good looks θ_{Ti}.

Data for our empirical tests come from Smith (2005), and were originally compiled in January 2003 from ratemyprofessors.com, a website dedicated to rating the quality of instruction (pedagogical productivity) in higher education that is available to college/university students from across the United States. Individual faculty represent the unit of observation. An individual faculty member was placed in the sample only if he/she had 10 or more student ratings (Cashin, 1995). The website was essentially scoured for all faculty with 10 or more ratings (Smith, 2005). For the few schools with hundreds of faculty with 10 or more ratings, a random subset (of up to 200 faculty) was chosen from that school. The final sample includes 2,986 individual faculty. Q_{Ti} is proxied by indicators of teaching effectiveness that come from the web site.[6] These are EASE, HELP, CLEAR, and QUALITY, and they represent mean ratings (from a 1 to 5 rating scale) earned by professors in the sample across the areas of easiness/difficulty, helpfulness, clarity and overall quality of instruction. θ_{Ti} is proxied by the variable LOOKS, which is the proportion of student evaluators who rate a given professor as attractive/sexy. It is expected that an aptitude for high-quality teaching would, *ceteris paribus*, create a tendency for employment at a liberal arts college or university, given that teaching is the primary source of advancement (promotion), tenure, and financial rewards at these institutions. Therefore, we expect HELP, CLEAR and QUALITY to be positively related to *prob*(LIBARTS=1), where

"LIBARTS" replaces "Z" from the discussion above. Given its survey construction, EASE is expected to be negatively related to *prob*(LIBARTS=1). Support for our hypothesis concerning attractiveness/good looks and institutional setting is found by a positive and significant coefficient attached to LOOKS. These relationships are explored empirically below.

3. Empirical Results

Summary statistics for our variables are provided in Table 1. About 8.6 percent of the sample of 2,986 individual faculty is represented by individuals employed by

Table 1
Variable Definitions and Summary Statistics

Variable Name	Definition	Mean	Standard Deviation
LIBARTS	Dummy variable equal to 1 for faculty located at liberal arts institutions, and 0 otherwise.	0.086	0.280
EASE	Average rating for each faculty based on course rigor, using a 1 (difficult) to 5 (easy) rating.	3.025	0.821
HELP	Average rating for each faculty based on willingness of faculty to offer out-of-class assistance to students, using a 1 (not helpful) to 5 (helpful) scale.	3.529	0.956
CLEAR	Average rating for each faculty based on clarity of lecture or instruction in learning, using a 1 (not clear) to 5 (clear) scale.	3.445	0.981
QUALITY	Average rating of the overall quality of each faculty; calculated as the average of HELP and CLEAR.	3.490	0.956
LOOKS	The proportion of students that indicate a particular faculty as being physically attractive/good-looking.	0.059	0.156

Data source: Smith (2004). Data originally compiled from ratemyprofessors.com.

liberal arts colleges. Also, the mean for LOOKS is 0.059, indicating that on average only about six percent of student respondents rate an individual professor as attractive/good-looking.

Five versions of a logistic regression model of equation (3) are presented in Table 2, each of which passes the usual joint significance test. The academic quality proxies all are correctly signed, and, in most cases, are significant at the 0.01 level. In version (1), HELP is positive and significant at the 0.10 level.

Table 2
Logistic Regression Results
dependent variable: LIBARTS

Regressors	(1)	(2)	(3)	(4)
constant	-2.343*	-2.310*	-2.256*	-2.325*
	(-7.73)	(-7.69)	(-7.63)	(-7.70)
EASE	-0.623*	-0.613*	-0.584*	-0.621*
	(-6.20)	(-6.14)	(-5.98)	(-6.18)
	[-0.049]	[-0.048]	[-0.046]	[-0.049]
HELP	0.343‡			0.483*
	(1.74)			(5.29)
	[0.027]			[0.038]
CLEAR	0.149		0.442*	
	(0.79)		(5.06)	
	[0.012]		[0.035]	
QUALITY		0.477*		
		(5.23)		
		[0.037]		
LOOKS	0.676†	0.689†	0.723†	0.701†
	(1.79)	(1.82)	(1.92)	(1.86)
	[0.053]	[0.054]	[0.057]	[0.055]
nobs	2,986	2,986	2,986	2,986
Model χ^2	53.58*	52.30*	50.57*	52.95*

Notes: The numbers in parentheses above are *t*-values, where *(†)[‡] denote the 0.01(0.075)[0.10] level of significance. The numbers in brackets are marginal probability estimates for the regressors (i.e., $[\partial \text{Prob}(\text{LIBARTS}=1)]/\partial x$]).

These results indicate that those professors exhibiting attributes of high-quality teaching, such as an ability to deliver lectures with clarity, a willingness to spend time outside of class assisting students in their studies, a desire to offer more rigorous course requirements, and/or an ability to offer a high overall level of teaching quality, are more likely than others to retain employment at liberal arts institutions. We argue that this is because their teaching efforts/talents will be more highly valued/rewarded at institutions that focus more on teaching (i.e., liberal arts) than research; that is, incentives matter.

The positive/significant result for LOOKS indicates that faculty who are perceived to be attractive are also more likely to retain employment at a liberal arts college/university, *ceteris paribus*. This is so, as we contend, because (1) beauty plays an important role in the teaching component of each professor's productivity matrix, and (2) the returns to teaching-related productivity are higher at liberal arts institutions. Lastly, the marginal probabilities on the LOOKS coefficients are sizable, ranging from 0.053 to 0.057 (see Caudill and Jackson, 1989). These findings are strongly supportive of our hypotheses and the results in Hamermesh and Biddle (1998), and in Hamermesh and Parker (2003).

One possible limitation of our interpretation of the results above is that each professor's teaching productivity and each professor's physical appearance are being evaluated by the same group. Even though correlations among individuals' ratings of attractiveness are very high, to the extent that students are pleased with a professor's performance, it is possible that they will rate him/her high on everything, including attractiveness (Hamermesh and Biddle, 1994; Boex, 2000; Hamermesh, 2004).[7] Therefore, students may be likely to over- or under-rate a professor's looks as they complete a teaching productivity questionnaire.

To deal with this issue, we first examined the Pearson correlation coefficients between LOOKS and our four measures of teaching productivity (i.e., EASE, HELP, CLEAR, QUALITY). Surprisingly, these coefficients are relatively small (see Table 3), ranging in size from about 0.16 to about 0.32. These correlations suggest that the extent to which students' ratings of professors' looks is affected by their ratings of professors' teaching style/quality is relatively small. Second, to further parse this issue we estimated equation (4) below by OLS:

$$(4) \ LOOKS = \alpha + \delta_1 EASE + \delta_2 HELP + \delta_3 CLEAR + \delta_4 EASE^2 + \delta_5 HELP^2 + \beta_6 CLEAR^2 + \varepsilon_{LOOKS}.$$

Equation (4) uses students' ratings of each professor's teaching productivity to predict their ratings of his/her physical beauty (with squared terms included to increase explanatory power). The error term in this equation (ε_{LOOKS}) approximates each professor's attractiveness rating not accounted for by his/her teaching performance. As such, ε_{LOOKS} is taken to represent each professor's true attractiveness rating.

Next we examined the correlation statistics between this adjusted attractiveness rating, ε_{LOOKS}, and the four measures of teaching productivity. These correlations are presented in Table 3, and are all at or very near zero. Whatever correlation existed between LOOKS and the four teaching productivity measures is removed when ε_{LOOKS} replaces LOOKS in the correlation matrix. Finally, using the same logistic choice method as in equation (3), we regressed LIBARTS on the teaching productivity measures and ε_{LOOKS} (i.e., the difference between LOOKS and the fitted values for LOOKS from equation (4) above). Table 4 presents the coefficient estimates for ε_{LOOKS}, following the same specification format used in Table 2. In each case, ε_{LOOKS} is positive and significant. The parameter estimates and marginal effects are only slightly smaller than their

Table 3
Additional Empirical Tests for Ratings (In)Dependence

	Pearson Correlation Matrix			
	EASE	HELP	CLEAR	QUALITY
LOOKS	0.1596	0.3198	0.3247	0.3271
ε_{LOOKS}	0.0164	0.0115	0.0090	0.0092
	Additional Logistic Regression Estimates			
	Table 2, Version (1)	Table 2, Version (2)	Table 2, Version (3)	Table 2, Version (4)
ε_{LOOKS}	0.650‡	0.657‡	0.665‡	0.654‡
	(1.68)	(1.69)	(1.70)	(1.69)
	[0.051]	[0.052]	[0.052]	[0.051]

Notes: The numbers in parentheses above are *t*-values associated with the ε_{LOOKS} parameter estimates. ‡ denotes significance at the 0.10 level. The numbers in brackets are marginal probability estimates for ε_{LOOKS} (i.e., $[\partial \text{Prob}(\text{LIBARTS}=1)]/\partial \varepsilon_{LOOKS}$). The full regression results employing the ε_{LOOKS} substitution are not presented here for brevity, but are comparable to those using LOOKS (i.e., those in Table 2).

Table 2 counterparts using LOOKS. In effect, these tests parse the *ratings (in)dependence* issue raised in Boex (2000) and Hamermesh (2004). They also provide added support for the hypothesis that beauty plays a significant role in occupational choices in higher education.

4. Concluding Comments

Much like Hamermesh and Parker (2003), this study does not address whether the relationship between attractiveness and student evaluations of teaching effectiveness represents pedagogical productivity or customer discrimination. This ongoing debate is of little relevance to the present study. In fact, we take the exhibited positive and statistically significant relationship between an instructor's appearance and his/her course evaluations as a given. In addition, we accept that, whether or not instructor ratings represent productivity, university administrators behave as if they do in promotion/tenure and raise determination processes. We merely posit that, other things constant, attractive professors are more likely to be employed at liberal arts institutions, because the teaching component receives greater importance in the promotion, tenure, and raise determination processes in these types of institutional settings than they do at research-oriented universities (i.e., incentives matter). Using indicators of teaching effectiveness and attractiveness from a large, well-known Internet-based service, findings from a logit model of occupational choice are consistent with our hypothesis.

Notes

* The authors thank Daniel Hamermesh, James Felton, and Kenneth Smith for helpful comments. We are also grateful to Kenneth Smith for providing the data, and to Subhashish Sengupta for data assistance. Any errors are our own.

1. See Hamermesh and Biddle (1994) and Hatfield and Sprecher (1986) on the empirical consistency of perceived attractiveness/beauty (θ) at a point in time.

2. For example, administrators at U.S. colleges and universities typically seek to index teaching productivity with formalized student evaluations of teaching. Research productivity is often indexed by documenting the quantity and quality of each professor's journal publications and books, as well as by counting the citations to an individual's published scholarship. Likewise, indexing service contributions involves documentation of committee, professional and community service work.

3. Some studies have also shown the existence of a "halo effect," where attractive instructors can partly avoid the damaging consequences of classroom rigor that often motivate less attractive instructors to implement less rigorous

standards and pursue grade inflation (Krautmann and Sander, 1999; Boex, 2000; Bosshardt and Watts, 2001; Felton, Mitchell and Stinson, 2004; Smith, 2005). The education/psychology literature is also replete with studies identifying the "fox" and "halo" effects in higher education.

4. Hamermesh and Parker (2003) point out that, regardless of the statistical evidence or one's beliefs about whether student evaluations have any relation to pedagogical productivity, instructional ratings/evaluations by students are part of what universities use in their evaluation of faculty teaching performance. Thus, even if instructional ratings/evaluations have little (or nothing) to do with actual teaching productivity, university administrators behave as if they believe they do. This leads administrators to link economic rewards to formal student evaluations.

5. U.S. college and university classifications are often used by accrediting agencies (Carnegie, etc.) and can be found in college guides, such as *U.S. News & World Report's America's Best Colleges* series. Employment descriptions of the various job listings in the American Economic Association's *Job Openings for Economists* provides concise anecdotal evidence as to the various missions and expectations of faculty at liberal arts versus comprehensive research universities.

6. As Smith (2005) indicates, this web site is freely accessible, and anyone can rate a professor. Thus, the data are clearly not gathered in a scientific manner. However, the web site does represent a standardized rating system that can be compared across different institutional types, and it offers the only large sample source of data of this kind (at present). Therefore, we proceed with caution to our empirical analysis.

7. We are grateful to Daniel Hamermesh for suggesting this avenue of discussion.

References

Becker, W.E. and M. Watts (1999) "How departments of economics evaluate teaching," *American Economic Review* 90: 355-359.

Biddle, J.E. and D.S. Hamermesh (1998) "Beauty, productivity and discrimination: Lawyers' looks and lucre," *Journal of Labor Economics* 16: 172-201.

Boex, L.F. (2000) "Attributes of effective economics instructors: An analysis of student evaluations," *Journal of Economic Education* 31: 211-227.

Bosshardt, W. and M. Watts (2001) "Comparing student and instructor evaluations of teaching," *Journal of Economic Education* 32: 3-17.

Cashin, W.E. (1995) "Student ratings of teaching: The research revisited," Center for Faculty Evaluation and Development, Kansas State University.

Caudill, S.B. and J.D. Jackson (1989) "Measuring marginal effects in limited-dependent variable models," *The Statistician* 38: 203-206.

Felton, J., J. Mitchell, and M. Stinson (2004) "Web-based student evaluations of professors: The relations between perceived quality, easiness, and sexiness," *Assessment & Evaluation in Higher Education* 29: 91-108.

Hamermesh, D.S. (2004) "Subjective outcomes in economics," *Southern Economic Journal* 71: 2-11.

Hamermesh, D.S. and J.E. Biddle (1994) "Beauty and the labor market," *American Economic Review* 84: 1,174-1,194.

—————, X. Meng, and J. Zhang (2002) "Dress for success: Does primping pay?" *Labour Economics* 9: 361-373.

————— and A.M. Parker (2003) "Beauty in the classroom: Professors' pulchritude and putative pedagogical productivity," Unpublished Manuscript.

Hatfield, E. and S. Sprecher (1986) *Mirror, mirror...: The importance of looks in everyday life*, Albany, NY: State University of New York Press.

Katz, D. (1973) "Faculty salaries, promotions, and productivity at a large university," *American Economic Review* 37: 592-606.

Kaun, D. (1984) "Faculty advancement in a nontraditional university environment," *Industrial and Labor Relations Review* 37: 592-606.

Krautmann, A.C. and W. Sander (1999) "Grades and student evaluations of teachers," *Economics of Education Review* 18: 59-63.

Moore, W.J., R. Newman and G. Turnbull (1998) "Do academic salaries decline with seniority?" *Journal of Labor Economics* 16: 352-366.

Pfann, G.A., J.E. Biddle, D.S. Hamermesh and C.M. Bosman (2000) "Business success and businesses' beauty capital," *Economics Letters* 67: 201-207.

Siegfried, J. and K. White (1973) "Financial rewards to research and teaching: A case study of academic economists," *American Economic Review* 63: 309-315.

Smith, K. (2005) "Getting econometrics students to evaluate student evaluations," in *Shaping the learning curve: Essays on economic education*, edited by Franklin G. Mixon, Jr., New York: iUniverse, Inc.

Part II.

Teaching and Content

6

Teaching Economic Development as a Part of International Economics
A Survey of Methods and a Suggested Pedagogy

W. CHARLES SAWYER AND RICHARD L. SPRINKLE

I. Introduction

To one extent or another, many of the subject areas in economics are a mixture of two or more major fields within economics. An example of this approach is the area of development economics. This area is a mixture of microeconomics, macroeconomics, international economics, public finance and other areas. In this case, the purpose of this mixture is to analyze economic problems in the context of developing countries. Regional economics uses a similar approach to the study of regions within a particular country. In a similar vein, the area of international economics uses a variety of areas of economics to analyze economic relations among countries.

In the case of international economics, it can be divided into two major areas: international trade and international finance. The subject area of international trade typically studies trade patterns among countries. However, there is more to this subject area than just studying trade patterns of countries. Along with the usual study of comparative advantage and the factor proportions theory of trade, there are a number of other topics normally covered in the first half of an international economics course. International trade is rarely free of obstructions, so tariff and nontariff barriers to trade typically are described and analyzed in this part of the course. Much of the thrust of international trade negotiations concerns dismantling barriers to trade. Explaining this process involves a study of the GATT/WTO negotiating process. With the increasing number of regional trade agreements (RTAs), a discussion of their role has become an increasingly important part of international trade. Recently, courses in international economics have emphasized the role of public choice in the analysis of trade agreements. Finally, the international movement of labor and capital have received increased emphasis in international trade as these movements may be substitutes for international trade in goods and services.

The subject area of international finance within an international economics course normally has three major components. The first component is a discussion and analysis of the balance of payments. The purpose of this component is to decompose and explain the inflows and outflows of domestic currency (money) to and from the rest of the world. The second component is how exchange rates are determined. The basic purpose of this analysis is to explain the determination of nominal exchange rates and what causes them to change. In most cases, exchange rate analysis also includes an explanation of purchasing power parity and the real exchange rate. The final component is open economy macroeconomics. Given the increased interdependence of countries, interaction with the rest of the world now impacts the macroeconomic dynamics of a country. This part of an international economics course usually supplements what students have already learned in either principles of macroeconomics or intermediate macroeconomics.

The above description of an international economics course illustrates the initial point that the study of international economics is a blend of topics in some of the various fields of economics. However, something deliberately has been left out of this description. International economics and economic development are in some senses closely related parts of economics. Both subject areas deal with global economic issues. Further, international trade and international finance topics are usually incorporated into any course in economic development. In addition, it is now quite common to cover some economic development topics in an international economics course. An international economics course or textbook that did not attempt to cover some economic development topics would look "peculiar." The issue is: How to discuss and analyze economic development topics in an international economics course or textbook. One approach would be to interweave the discussion of the developing countries in an international economics course at various points in the course or textbook when this is appropriate.[1] However, the more standard approach is to incorporate the economic development material as one or two chapters within a textbook or one or two lectures within a course which analyzes various international trade and international finance aspects of economic development. It is this second approach that is the starting point of this paper. In the next section, we will review the coverage of economic development in a number of standard international economics texts. In the following two sections, we offer alternative methods of teaching both international trade and finance in the context of developing countries. A concluding section summarizes the paper and offers suggestions on other alternatives to teaching economic development within an international economics course.

2. The Coverage of Economic Development in Existing Textbooks

Most, though not all, international economics textbooks contain some coverage of economic development topics. In this section, we review the coverage of economic development in international economics books that have been through a minimum of four editions. These books include Carbaugh (2004), Husted and Melvin (2004), Kreinin (2002), Krugman and Obstfeld (2003), Pugel (2004), Salvatore (2004), and Yarbrough and Yarbrough (2002). As noted above, a complete coverage of economic development would require two separate sections. One would concern international trade and the other would cover international finance. As we will see, such complete coverage is rare in the existing international economics textbooks.

The coverage of economic development in international economics books is summarized in Table 1. The first column lists the various textbooks mentioned above. The second column contains a summary of topics covered in the chapters or sections of each textbook covering international trade and economic development. The third column contains a summary of which textbooks contain an international finance chapter or section on economic development, and, if so, which topics are covered.

Five out of the seven textbooks contain chapters on international trade and economic development. Only Husted and Melvin (2004) does not have a separate chapter on the general topic. Many of these textbooks contain one or more of four common themes. The first theme is some sort of listing of problems that developing countries encounter with respect to international trade. For economists trained in the 1970s and 1980s, these problems are familiar. The topics include low commodity prices; the alleged declining terms of trade for developing countries; and market access problems. A second common theme is a description of the multilateral institutions providing official development assistance. Included in these institutions are the World Bank, the WTO, and the United Nations Conference on Trade and Development (UNCTAD). The third and most common theme now is a discussion of trade strategies and economic growth. The usual coverage of this topic concerns the difference between import substitution and export promotion strategies. A final theme is international trade and economic growth put into a more technical framework. The usual coverage involves explaining the process of

Table 1
Summary of Economic Development Coverage in International Economics Textbooks

Textbook (year)	International Trade and Economic Development	International Finance and Economic Development
Carbaugh (2004)	Trade Problems Generalized System of Preferences Commodity Prices Growth Strategies	No Chapter
Husted and Melvin (2004)	One-half of a chapter on Growth Strategies	Section of a chapter on IMF Conditionality
Kreinin (2002)	Growth Strategies International Institutions	No Chapter
Krugman and Obstfeld (2003)	Growth Strategies Debt Problems	Financial Crisis
Pugel (2004)	Growth Strategies	Financial Crisis
Salvatore (2004)	Terms of Trade Growth Strategies	No Chapter
Yarbrough & Yarbrough (2002)	One-third of a chapter on Economic Growth	One-half of a chapter on Macroeconomics

economic growth as an accumulation of capital and labor and how international trade or the migration of factors of production can influence this process.

In contrast to the coverage of international trade is the coverage of international finance in these textbooks. In relation to the coverage of international trade, the coverage of international finance is meager. Three out of the seven books listed in Table 1 do not have a section on international finance and economic development. In addition, one of the other textbooks has only a brief section on a single international finance topic (IMF conditionality). Given the growing emphasis on international finance issues in the world economy, this lack of coverage is puzzling. Further, the range of topics in the textbooks that do have a separate chapter on international finance is extremely limited. One of the four books has a chapter that primarily covers international financial institutions such as the IMF. Of the other three books that have an international finance chapter, there is a striking uniformity. There is essentially one topic covered by all three books. This topic is financial crises in developing countries. The coverage normally includes a list of recent crises in developing countries. This listing is supplemented by a discussion of debt problems and the role of the IMF in developing countries.

The coverage of economic development in these textbooks indicates several things about the way the subject matter is integrated into international economics courses. First, international trade and economic development is much more heavily covered than international finance. Second, the coverage of international trade and economic development is not uniform across textbooks. This lack of uniformity in topic coverage is unlike the other topics in international trade, where there is virtually a template on how to cover certain topics such as comparative advantage or the analysis of tariffs. Third, the coverage of international finance and economic development is much less developed than the coverage of international trade. In the next two sections, we will offer some suggestions on both areas that are designed to improve the coverage of economic development in international economics courses.

3. Teaching International Trade and Economic Development

Reviewing the information in Table 1 reveals an interesting fact about how the relationship between international trade and economic development is presented in most textbooks. In most chapters on this subject, there really is not much information on how international trade affects a country's economic growth. The heart of this subject in the context of economic development is how to increase a country's GDP per capita. If GDP per capita is rising, then this is usually used as a proxy for economic development. There are many other issues involved with economic development, but increasing GDP per capita is the most important issue. From the outset what is missing is how international trade affects economic growth, and, by extension, GDP per capita. In contrast, the material covered in some textbooks concerns trade policy, or the terms of trade, or international institutions such as the WTO. In this section, we will suggest a more systematic way of incorporating economic development into the international trade part of an international economics course.

The Developing Countries

Economic development and trade normally are covered at the end of the international trade part of the course. Since economic development is a new topic, the first task is to define the area of economic development. This involves discussing the multifaceted nature of this area of economics. Since it is impossible to cover all of the areas of economic development, it is clear that the material will focus on the relationship between international trade and GDP per capita. This simplification reduces the discussion of this relationship to a manageable amount of material. The next step is to put the developing countries in the context of the world economy. The objective of this discussion is to illustrate that the developing countries contain the majority of the world's population, but a minority of the world's income. This relationship between population and income illustrates why the topic is important in an international context. To further reinforce this point, the developing countries can be split into middle- and low-income countries. Comparing GDP per capita in these two types of developing countries to GDP per capita in high-income countries starkly shows why economic development is a critically important subject. Finally, by focusing on GDP per capita, the student can be led into the subject of how international trade can be used to increase the rate of growth of GDP.

Economic Growth

In explaining the effects of international trade on economic growth, the main device used is the standard neoclassical theory of economic growth. However, before the neoclassical model can be used, there are some assumptions the model makes that need to be discussed. It is now commonplace to consider two preconditions that are necessary before applying standard growth theory to a country. First, there must be mechanisms in place within a country to assure property rights. Free markets cannot work unless it is clear who owns what. Second, there must be some level of adherence to the rule of law. Consumers and businesses cannot function in an environment of widespread lawlessness. This discussion of preconditions also has another point. Many of the world's poorest countries are not growing very fast. In most cases, this occurs because the government has failed to enforce property rights or cannot maintain a legal environment necessary for economic growth.

Once these preconditions are understood, the neoclassical theory of economic growth can be introduced. This is relatively easy to explain using a standard production function as shown in Figure 1. Real GDP is shown on the vertical axis and the quantity of labor is given on the horizontal axis. Drawing on the discussion of the factors of production used in explaining the factor-proportions theory of international trade, it can be explained that capital is assumed for the moment to be constant. Further, the level of technology also is assumed to be constant. From Figure 1, one can illustrate two things. First, the production function takes its characteristic shape from the concept of diminishing returns. As ever greater amounts of labor are added to a given stock of capital and level of technology, then past some point the rate of increase in real GDP falls. Second, one can use

Figure 1: A Production Function for a Country

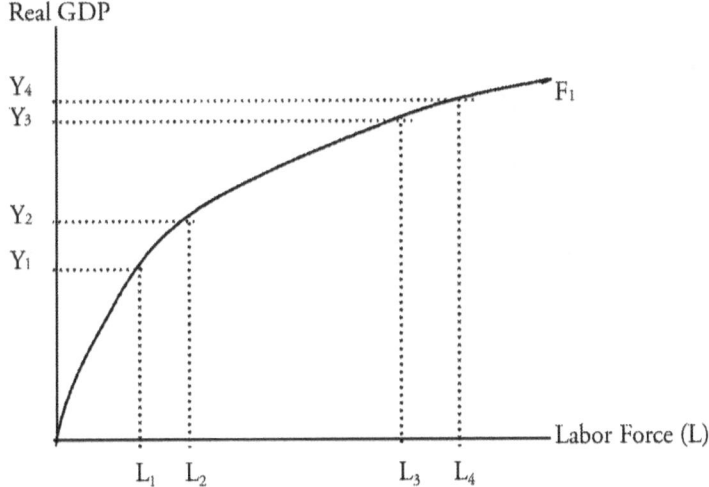

Figure 1 to illustrate why poor countries can grow faster than rich countries. At low levels of real GDP (Y_1) adding the same amount of labor yields a higher rate of growth of GDP (movement to Y_2) than it does for a country with a high level of real GDP (movement from Y_3 to Y_4). This is particularly important for developing countries. Not only is the level of real GDP closer to the origin, but the rate of growth of the labor force in a developing country is usually faster than it is in a high-income country.

One can now consider how changes in the stock of capital and the level of technology affect economic growth. If the capital stock increases, then the production function will shift upwards as shown in Figure 2. For any given level of employment (labor), more real GDP is produced (Y_1 to Y_2). Again, one can relate the discussion back to the factor-proportions theory. In this model, the capital-to-labor ratio (K/L) was an important variable. As the stock of capital rises, the K/L rises, and real GDP rises. Figure 2 can also be used to show how increases in the level of technology increase real GDP. A rising level of technology shifts the production function upwards and increases real GDP. This explanation of basic growth theory is sufficient to set the stage for how international trade increases economic growth.

Figure 2: A Shift in the Production Function for a Country

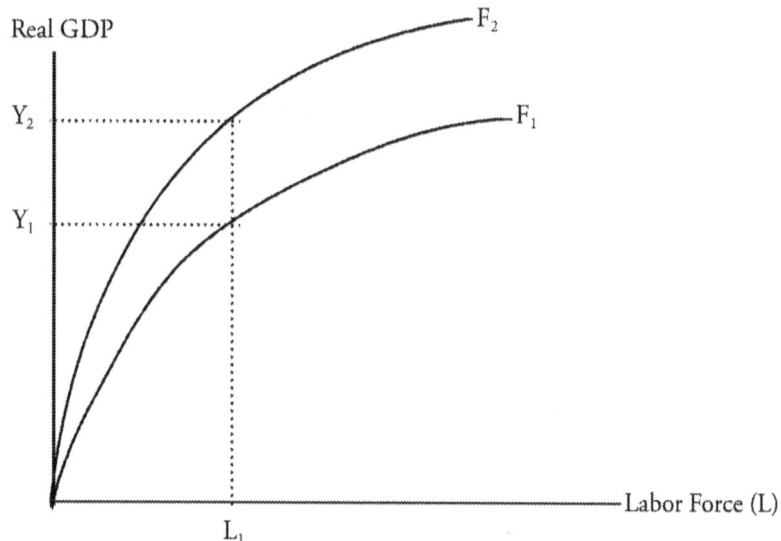

International Trade and Economic Growth

It is conventional wisdom in international economics that international trade will increase the rate of economic growth. The positive relationship (correlation) between openness and growth is well established.[2] However, the exact linkages between trade and growth still are being established. One of the more obvious changes is that trade increases the productivity of resources used in the economy. In an international economics course, the students already know this. In covering comparative advantage, students are shown that trade would move resources from comparative disadvantage to comparative advantage industries. This process increases the total output of the economy because resources in a comparative advantage industry are more productive than resources in a comparative disadvantage industry. All that remains is to put this insight into the context of economic growth.

Moving resources from comparative disadvantage to comparative advantage industries increases the output of the economy. In terms of growth theory, this increases the total factor productivity of the economy. Although technology is a difficult thing to measure, total factor productivity can be measured. In this case, total factor productivity increases can be seen as a useful proxy for the level of technology. This allows one to make a more formal link between international trade and economic growth. It only remains to establish that there is a positive correlation between openness and total factor productivity. Fortunately, this is seen in the empirical work of Edwards (1998). Higher degrees of openness are associated with higher levels of economic growth. This is because an increasing amount of international trade tends to shift the production function upwards as a result of increases in total factor productivity.

Import Substitution vs. Export Promotion

At the end of the discussion on international trade and economic growth, one can use the production function to illustrate why a successful developing country can grow so fast. In a developing country, the labor force typically is growing at a rapid rate so economic growth is enhanced even without increases in the stock of capital or the level of technology. However, in most cases the production function also may be shifting upward at a rapid rate. The stock of capital may be increasing both due to the domestic accumulation of capital and foreign direct investment (FDI). This reinforces the importance of FDI that may have been covered earlier in the course. Further, the production function may be shifting upwards as the country's trade policy and the policies of the other countries are changing. The average level of tariffs in the world economy is falling. This makes it easier for countries to become more "open" by exporting more. It is also true that many developing countries are latecomers to the process of trade liberalization. By lowering their trade barriers, their economies become more open due to the process of increasing imports. These imports are important as they make the economy more efficient. Resources are driven out of comparative disadvantage industries into comparative advantage industries.

At this point, it becomes obvious why countries that have pursued a policy of promoting exports have been more successful than countries pursuing import substitution policies. Import substitution development policies consistently have failed to produce high levels of economic growth. Why this is so now can be shown graphically. These policies have tended to put resources into comparative disadvantage industries. The protection of these industries tends to put more of an economy's resources in these industries. These industries grow faster but this growth carries a price. Putting more resources in comparative disadvantage industries reduces the overall output of the economy. Over time, however, the production function does not shift upwards as fast and economic growth for the country is lower. Aside from any other issues associated with import substitution, economic growth is hindered in countries that can ill afford low economic growth. A strategy of export promotion works in reverse. These policies would tend to encourage the movement of resources into comparative advantage industries.

This movement would increase total factor productivity and shift the production function upwards at a faster rate. The discussion of import substitution versus export promotion can now be put on a firmer basis. Rather than just discussing the institutional details of the two strategies, the instructor can now "show" students the difference between the two in a way firmly grounded in both the theory of international economics and the neoclassical theory of economic growth.

4. Capital Flows and Economic Development

In an international economics course the issue of capital flows and economic development is a relatively new topic. In the 21st Century, this is peculiar. Much of what students hear about developing countries concerns a financial crisis in one or more countries. International economics textbooks have responded to this reality by adding a chapter in the international finance section of the course. However, in most cases the discussion is institutional or historical. The student may learn some of the terms and a bit of economic history, but not much analysis. In the end, students may still not understand the role of capital flows in the economic development of a country or why these flows can cause economic problems for developing countries. This section of the paper offers a methodology to equip students to better understand what they hear or read about capital flows and the developing countries. The advantage of this methodology is that it only requires that the students understand basic exchange rate determination and aggregate demand/aggregate supply analysis.

The Reasons for Capital Flows to Developing Countries

In teaching this subject, the instructor needs to explain why capital is flowing from the high-income countries to the developing countries. Once again, the instructor can use the factor-proportions theory to explain this movement. High-income countries are normally capital abundant. As a group, the developing countries are labor abundant. By definition, this means that developing countries are capital scarce relative to the high-income countries. This has implications for the rate of return to capital. The return on capital usually will be low in the capital-abundant high-income countries. On the other hand, the return to capital in the developing countries usually will be high. In the absence of barriers to the flow of capital, capital in the world economy will tend to flow from high-income countries to the developing countries. The form of these flows is important and is the subject of the next section.

Debt vs. Equity

Many students in an international economics need to learn, or at least review, the concepts of debt and equity. Since capital is scarce in developing countries, the government or private sector enterprises may borrow money from lenders in the high-income countries. Further, they may borrow money from multilateral lending institutions such as the World Bank. The total of this borrowing by a country constitutes its debt to the rest of the world. While this process is a normal part of economic development, debt repayment can be troublesome. The most important characteristic of debt is that payments of interest or principal must be made at certain points in time. In this case, the financial condition of the borrower is an issue. If the borrower cannot make all of the debt payments at a particular point in time, then the borrower may have to default on some of the loan repayments. While there is conceptually nothing wrong with borrowing to finance economic development, the lenders must be careful about monitoring the extent of a country's borrowing. A second way to create capital inflows is the use of equity. Equity is where the lender is involved in the ownership and management of the investment. A common form of equity finance is foreign direct investment. Another form of equity is the movement of capital into the financial markets of developing countries to purchase common stock. The important characteristic of equity is that the return on equity does not have to be paid at specific points in time.

An important distinction can be made at this point. For a country, debt is much riskier than equity. A large stock of debt obligates a country to make payments on this debt in a foreign currency at specific time periods. To make prompt payment, the country must have a sufficient amount of foreign exchange at particular points in time. If the amount of foreign exchange is inadequate, then the country may have to default on some of its debts. This risk is related to two variables. First, the absolute size of a country's foreign exchange reserves is important. Debt repayment becomes much riskier if the size of these foreign exchange reserves is small. A related concept is the debt/export ratio. This ratio relates the country's debt payments to its earnings of foreign exchange from its exports. If either of these variables is low then this is a warning to both the government of the country and potential foreign lenders. Debt repayment problems do not usually materialize overnight, but may develop over time. The occasional spectacle of a country defaulting on its debt may be a surprise to the casual observer, but it is not usually a surprise to international financial markets. The problem with capital flows into developing countries is not necessarily the total amount of capital flows. It is usually a problem to too much of the flow being in the form of debt relative to equity.

Exchange Rate Shocks

Once a student understands the difference between debt and equity, a financial crisis in a developing country becomes more understandable. What now can be explained is the process that frequently leads to the accumulation of a substantial amount of debt in a developing country. The best way to describe this can be seen in Figure 3. This figure shows the demand and supply for foreign exchange and the market equilibrium exchange rate at XR_e. Another exchange rate is shown in the Figure. XR_f is the exchange rate that has been fixed by government. This exchange rate is below the market equilibrium and has predictable consequences. At this exchange rate, the demand for foreign exchange is "A" and the supply of foreign exchange is "B". The difference between exports and imports equals a country's current account deficit. The only remaining question is how this current account deficit is being "financed."

If the financing involves inflows of equity capital, all is well. FDI and to a lesser extent portfolio investment are not likely to leave a country quickly. These capital inflows would shift the supply of foreign exchange from S to S'. As such, these inflows would make the fixed exchange rate sustainable. Unfortunately, there is another way this shift in supply of foreign exchange could occur. The government could borrow foreign exchange in the international capital markets to be able to supply the amount of foreign exchange necessary to maintain the exchange rate. This is a sustainable strategy so long as international lenders can be found to make the loans. However, if this borrowing becomes impossible, then the supply of foreign exchange may shift abruptly to the left. In this case, the country is forced to allow its currency to depreciate. Further, the inability to borrow may trigger a default on debt payments as the country now may not have sufficient foreign exchange to cover all debt repayments. What we have illustrated is a classic exchange rate shock.

While Figure 3 is instructive, it still does not convey to students why an exchange rate shock and accompanying default is such a calamity for a country. To explain this, one needs to employ some simple macroeconomic analysis using the aggregate demand/aggregate supply model students used in principles of economics. The aggregate demand/aggregate supply model is shown in Figure 4. The initial equilibrium is shown with the price level at P_e and real GDP at Y_e where the aggregate demand curve intersects the aggregate supply curve. The question is: What does an exchange rate shock do to the equilibrium level of output and price level of a country? In a developing country, imports typically are a high percentage of GDP. As the country's currency depreciates, the cost of imports increases by a relatively large amount. This affects the cost of production of practically all goods and services in the economy. In effect, the depreciation of

Figure 3: The Effect of an Exchange Rate Shock on the
Foreign Exchange Market

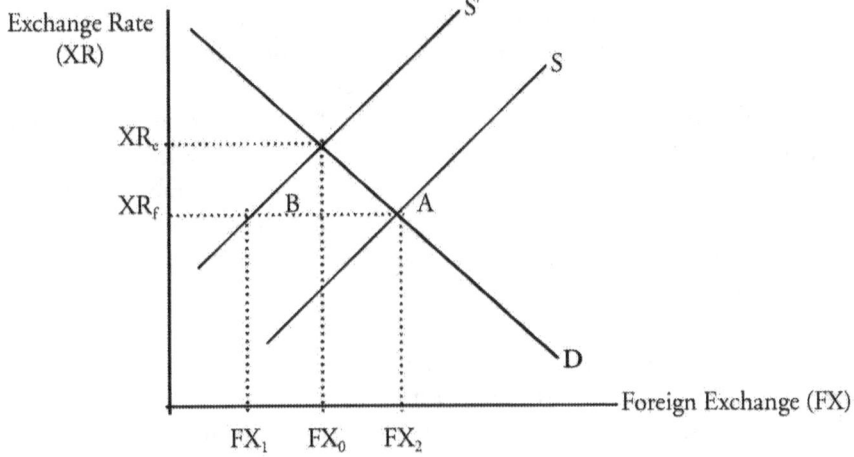

Figure 4: The Effect of an Exchange Rate Shock on the Economy

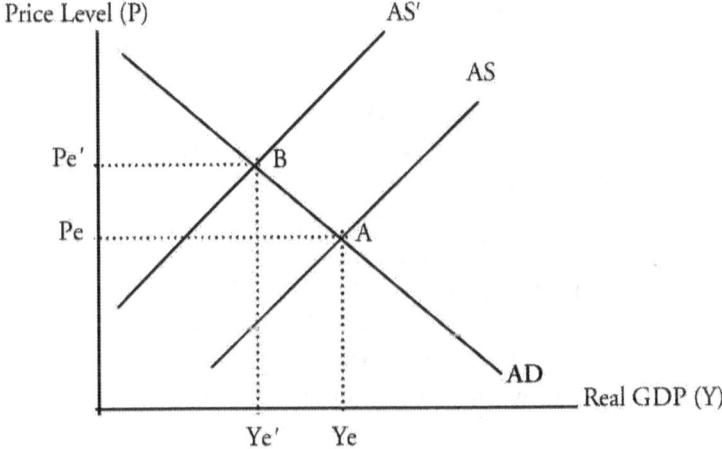

the country's currency affects the economy in much the same way that an oil
shock affects high-income countries. As the country's currency depreciates, the
aggregate supply curve (AS) shifts backwards and to the left. This movement in

the aggregate supply curve creates a new macroeconomic equilibrium. The price level rises from P_e to P_e' and real GDP falls from Y_e to Y_e'. These effects on output and prices would be uncomfortable in a high-income country. However, for a developing country, the effects can be much more serious.

First, as the new equilibrium illustrates, the rate of inflation in the country increases. Invariably, such a rise in prices causes a decline in real wages in the short run. If GDP per capita for a country is $25,000 a ten percent decline in the real wage would be an uncomfortable experience. However, for a developing country with a GDP per capita of $2,000, this decline is much more serious. In a country where absolute poverty is still a problem, this decline in real wages may well lead to malnutrition or in some cases starvation. In addition, the equilibrium level of GDP also declines. The decline in real GDP likewise is a more serious problem in a developing country. In virtually any country, a fall in real GDP leads to an increase in unemployment or underemployment. Increases in unemployment are a much more serious problem in countries that are too poor to afford social safety nets. Without widespread unemployment compensation or social welfare programs, a rise in the unemployment rate may result in more serious hardship than would be the case in a developed country. Further, the labor force usually is growing faster in developing countries than it is in developed countries. A fall in real GDP that lasts for any extended period of time may lead to a faster increase in the unemployment rate in a country where the labor force is growing rapidly than in a country where this growth is naturally slower.

Students can now better appreciate the use of the term crisis when referring to these events. A financial problem that leads to a depreciation of a country's currency can have serious consequences for a developing country. The standard of living in a country where GDP per capita is already low falls even further. The problem is compounded by the difficulty that the governments of developing countries have in dealing with this sort of crisis. In the first place, the government faces the usual dilemma of what to do in the face of an aggregate supply shock. Attempting to suppress the inflation will increase the severity of the decline in real GDP and make unemployment worse. Trying to maintain the level of real GDP will exacerbate the problem of inflation. Even if this decision to re-inflate the economy is undertaken, the macroeconomic tools to carry out the policy in a developing country are limited. Fiscal policy is difficult to use when government spending as a percentage of GDP is still low. Discretionary monetary policy is difficult to use in a developing country context. Manipulating the money supply in the absence of open market operations is not easy to do. A frequent policy response in a developing country is to simply print money to cover an expanding fiscal deficit. This response may reduce the adverse effect on real GDP but substantially increase the rate of inflation. At this point, students can be shown using

Figure 3 the impact of an increase in a country's rate of inflation on the value of its exchange rate over time. In this case, an exchange rate shock may lead to a cycle of loose monetary policy and a continually depreciating exchange rate in some developing countries.

The Role of the IMF

At this point, students invariably start thinking about the role of the IMF in exchange rate crises. In the public mind, a financial crisis and the IMF have become inextricably linked. Using Figures 3 and 4, the role of the IMF can be easily shown. First, in many situations a financial crisis has been averted by the IMF. Frequently, a country can forecast an upcoming financial crisis. If foreign reserves are falling in a country, with a bit of arithmetic one can determine a point when the country may not be able to make payments on all of its debt. At this point, the IMF becomes a lender of last resort. The IMF will loan the country the foreign exchange to avert a major depreciation of its currency. In exchange for the loan, the IMF will set conditions that are designed to make the exchange rate more sustainable and prevent a default on debt. These conditions may involve a slow depreciation of the country's currency. This approach is never popular as the price of imports in the country will rise. Second, the IMF may ask for changes in the country's macroeconomic policies. In general, the IMF usually requires the country to reduce its fiscal deficit and lower the rate of growth of the money supply. Tighter fiscal and monetary policy usually means a slower rate of economic growth and a higher rate of unemployment. Such measures may be necessary to reduce the country's need to borrow foreign exchange but they are not likely to be popular. Under these circumstances, it is small wonder that the IMF and its "conditionality" are deeply unpopular in developing countries.

5. Concluding Remarks

The purpose of this paper was to suggest a better way of incorporating the subject of economic development into an international economics course. Since international economics is split into two parts, this means that incorporating economic development is likewise split into two parts. Unfortunately, the current crop of international economics textbooks usually only cover international trade and economic development. The potential contribution of the material above is to show that economic development can easily be incorporated into both parts of an international economics course. Fortunately, economic development is usually one of the last topics covered in each part of the course. Using previously covered material makes it much easier to cover the economic development material.

If there is a trick in covering economic development in an international economics course, it is to ground the discussion of economic development in basic economic theory. All too often, the discussion of economic development bogs down in a morass of institutional and historical details. While interesting, these details are in many cases best left to a whole course in economic development. Students in international economics need to learn how international trade can increase the economic growth rate of the country. This is particularly important for developing countries, but also for any country. Using the basic theory of economic growth, how this occurs is fairly easy to teach. In the international finance section of the course, students need to learn why capital flows to developing countries and the different forms these flows can take. From this discussion, the potential problems with this process can be analyzed.

In teaching this material, it is useful to keep one overriding consideration in mind. Most of the students in an international economics course are not going to graduate school in economics. In most cases, their ultimate destination is a managerial job in the private or public sectors. To be more effective managers, they badly need to be able to understand the information on developing countries that they will encounter in the business press. The material presented above is designed to do just that. It is designed to give the students a simple framework for analyzing trade, capital flows, and economic development.

Notes

1.   For an example of this approach, see Sawyer and Sprinkle (2003).

2.   Openness is usually defined as the ratio of exports plus imports to GDP. For a survey on this issue, see Dollar and Kraay (2001).

References

Carbaugh, R. (2004) *International economics* (9th edition), Cincinnati, OH: South-Western.

Dollar, D. and A. Kraay (2001) "Trade, growth, and poverty," *Finance & Development* 38: 16-19.

Edwards, S. (1998) "Openness, productivity, and growth: What do we really know?" *Economic Journal* 108: 383-398.

Husted, S. and M. Melvin (2004) *International economics* (6th edition), Boston, MA: Addison-Wesley.

Kreinin, M.E. (2002) *International economics* (9th edition), Cincinnati, OH: South-Western.

Krugman, P.R. and M. Obstfeld (2003) *International economics* (6th edition), Boston, MA: Addison-Wesley.

Pugel, T.A. (2004) *International economics* (12th edition), Boston, MA: Irwin.

Salvatore, D. (2004) *International economics* (8th edition), New York, NY: John Wiley.

Sawyer, W.C. and R.L. Sprinkle (2003) *International economics*, Upper Saddle River, NJ: Prentice Hall.

Yarbrough, B.V. and R.M. Yarbrough (2002) *The world economy* (6th edition), Cincinnati, OH: Southwestern.

7

Cartels on Campus
The Case of the IFC and Panhellenic Council

STEVEN B. CAUDILL AND STEPHANIE A. HICKS

I. Introduction

Most students taking a microeconomics principles course are familiar with the idea of a cartel. In their principles text, Ekelund and Tollison (1997) describe a cartel as being, "an agreement among firms to restrict output in order to raise price and achieve monopoly power over a market." Ekelund and Tollison go on to describe a legal cartel as being, "supported by a law limiting entry and restricting competition among members." On many college campuses, fraternities and sororities have formed cartels to limit competition among members. The cartel is enforced, in the case of fraternities, by the Interfraternity Council, and, in the case of sororities, by the Panhellenic Council. The purpose of this essay is to associate these organizations with fraternity and sorority cartels, and to illustrate to principles of economics students how these organizations act to limit competition between fraternities and sororities for new members, or pledges.

There can be little doubt that college fraternities and sororities have formed successful cartels. Ekelund and Tollison (1997) list several factors contributing to cartel success, most of which are evidenced in campus Greek organizations.[1] Entry of new "firms" is difficult. Obtaining a charter to locate a new fraternity or sorority on campus is a slow and expensive process. Much effort is taken to homogenize "firm" output. Fraternities and sororities are social organizations, all selling their services at the same widely publicized price. All competition is non-price in nature. There are restrictions on the kind of amenities fraternity houses can offer (e.g., no swimming pools permitted at many universities, etc.). On some campuses, sororities are not permitted to have sorority houses and members live in specified sections of dormitories. There are no large buyers in the market. New members, or pledges, negotiate individually with fraternities and sororities. All of these factors add to the cartel power enjoyed by campus Greek organizations.

Fraternities and sororities are social organizations competing for pledges. The IFC and Panhellenic Council have established strict guidelines which have the effect of limiting competition between members for new pledges. Within the context of "limits to competition," these rules or guidelines are discussed, first for fraternities and then sororities.

2. Limits to Competition within the Campus Greek System

Fraternities and sororities are social organizations for college men and women, in competition (theoretically) with one another for new members, or pledges. Pledges are needed for the money and prestige they bring to the organization. The official time period for recruiting new members is known as "rush," which is the process of mutual preference and selection, where fraternities and sororities choose new members. Pre-rush is the period prior to Rush Week that involves orientation for sororities and a "Rush Fair" for fraternities.

During fraternity rush, a "rushee" may not be formally pledged until after the first day of formal rush. The agreement made by the colluding fraternities assures each fraternity an equal chance of pledging a highly sought-after rushee. Another rule limiting competition states that no fraternity man should slander or degrade another fraternity in the presence of a rushee. Nothing negative can be said about the "opposing firms." Colluding fraternities have also agreed to discontinue serving alcoholic beverages during the time specified as formal rush. This is another effort to limit competition. A third rule that the IFC enforces is that no fraternity should allow an orientation student (i.e., new student) to stay at its house during orientation period. Because the orientation period is a time for the person to gain a general view of the university, allowing the orientation student to stay with a particular fraternity would give that fraternity a competitive edge over other fraternities. Thus, observance of this rule by the IFC members diminishes competition. Members have also agreed not to hold parties at fraternity houses on the nights of the new student orientation period.

Sororities are governed by the Panhellenic Council. The Panhellenic Council sets rules and regulations which sororities agree upon to reduce competition during pre-rush and rush. During pre-rush, no written invitation may be issued and no planned entertainment may be held by a sorority. Chapter rooms may be used for guests on an individual basis only. Parties are not allowed.

Panhellenic has also established many rules for the pre-rush period. A prospective rushee, including relatives of sorority members, may not attend any organized sorority function where sorority members will be in attendance, such as lake parties, formals, or socials. In other words, a rushee cannot be involved in pre-rush recruiting. Also, no sorority members, pledges or alumnae may spend money on prospective rushees during the Summer before rush (or rush week). This would obviously give any one sorority an advantage in recruiting, especially if it has greater resources than other sororities.

Sororities are also constrained by many rules that ensure equal access to pledges. One such rule is that no alumnae may entertain a rushee during the Summer months or the rush week, encourage her to join a sorority, or put any undo pressure on her. At no time shall a sorority member discuss another sorority or one of its members in an unfavorable way. Alumnae and members' mothers may not converse with rushees during rush week. Beginning with the opening of residence halls for rush, rushees may not contact, or be contacted by, sorority members, pledges, alumnae or members' mothers in any way. And, under no circumstances may a member, pledge, alumnae, or member's mother indicate to a rushee that she will receive a bid from any sorority including her own, or say anything to indicate the rushee's status with a sorority.

There are many other regulations which help maintain the cartel. The following is a list of additional rules and regulations that apply to the actual rush week:

- Sorority members must stay in the chapter room while rushees are arriving for and leaving from rush parties.

- Sororities may not have any decorations during the Rotational Open Houses—no sorority song, chant or cheer may be performed.

- Only one item of food may be served during Preference parties.

- No name tags, gifts, flowers, or mementos are to be given to rushees.

- A particular skit theme may not be used by more than one sorority on the same day.

- A picture gallery and a slide show are allowed on only one day during rush.

- Alumnae and sorority members' mothers are not allowed to participate in any rush parties.

- Gifts are not allowed to be given on Preference Day, so that the recruiting process may be standardized.

- Sorority members are prohibited from wearing rush attire in public during formal rush period.

- There can be no decorations on a rushee's door during formal rush. Throughout the rush week, the lobby of the Panhellenic dorm may not be decorated with any sorority related items.

- Monetary limits are imposed on sororities during rush.

These rules, collectively, have the effect of limiting competition between members. As one can see, there are many rules which, if broken, would make sororities and fraternities more attractive to rushees. Therefore, there is support for the notion that fraternities and sororities collude to form councils to decrease competition, just as oligopolists collude to form cartels. One example similar to the one presented here is the National Collegiate Athletic Association, an organization discussed by Fleisher, Goff and Tollison (1992), Mixon (1996), and Barro (1997). Fleisher *et al.* (1992) state that economists generally view the NCAA as a cartel. They hold this view because the NCAA has historically devised rules to restrict output (e.g., the number of games played and televised) and to restrict competition for inputs (student athletes). They also point out that lenient antitrust policy provides a necessary condition for successful collusion.

3. Concluding Comments

In conclusion, the purpose of this paper is to show that college fraternities and sororities collude to form the IFC and Panhellenic Council, and thus appear to act as cartels. In the same manner that a cartel acts to limit competition, the IFC and Panhellenic Council establish many rules and regulations that also limit competition. Thus, their behavior provides a compelling example of real world cartel behavior that is visible to college students.

Note

1. For other work applying cartel theory/behavior to non-commercial activities, see Caudill and Mixon (1994), Chittom and Mixon (2003), Mixon (2001), and Mixon and Ressler (2001).

References

Barro, R.J. (1997) *Getting it right: Markets and choices in a free society*, Cambridge, MA: The MIT Press.

Caudill, S.B. and F.G. Mixon, Jr. (1994) "Cartels and the incentive to cheat: Evidence from the classroom," *Journal of Economic Education* 25: 267-269.

Chittom, A.B. and F.G. Mixon, Jr. (2003) "Do congressional leaders detect and deter cartel cheating? Evidence from committee assignments," *Economics of Governance* 4: 161-175.

Ekelund, R.B., Jr. and R.D. Tollison (1997) *Economics*, New York: Addison-Wesley.

Fleisher, A.A., III, B.L. Goff, and R.D. Tollison (1992) *The National Collegiate Athletic Association: A study in cartel behavior*, Chicago: University of Chicago Press.

McKeen, S.B. (1994) *Tonian*, Auburn: The Fraternite at Auburn University.

Mixon, F.G., Jr. (1996) "Legal cartels and social contracts: Lessons from the economic foundations of government," *International Journal of Social Economics* 23: 37-46.

Mixon, F.G., Jr. (2001) "Cartel (in)stability on *Survivor* island," *Journal of Education for Business* 77: 89-94.

Mixon, F.G., Jr. and R.W. Ressler (2001) "Loyal political cartels and committee assignments in Congress: Evidence from the Congressional Black Caucus," *Public Choice* 108: 313-330.

Poteat, C. (1994) *Tiger Cub*, Auburn: Student Handbook.

The Editors (1994) *Sorority Rush Handbook*, Auburn: Auburn University Printing.

8

Intraindustry Trade
A More Intuitive Metric

H. TYRONE BLACK

I. Introduction

International intraindustry trade (IIT) is the exchange of similar goods or services, such as "aircraft," during a given time period. IIT is an increasingly important component of trade in manufactured goods and some services (Sawyer and Sprinkle, 2003: 83-86). Several measures of intraindustry trade are available to summarize intraindustry trade at both the industry level and for a nation's aggregate intraindustry trade (see Grubel and Lloyd, 1975: chapter 2). The following **Grubel-Lloyd Index** (Grubel and Lloyd, 1975),

$$(1) \quad I = \left[1 - \left(\frac{|X - M|}{X + M} \right) \right] \times 100,$$

is a well-known formula for summarizing intraindustry trade at the industry level. With this index, intraindustry trade index values can range from a maximum of 100.00, when exports are equal to imports, to a minimum of 0.00, when either exports or imports are zero. A variation of the **Grubel-Lloyd Index** omits the 100 multiplier and thereby produces values that range from 0.00 to 1.00. This variation is most commonly used in international economics texts, and the discussion in the next section pertains to this version.

2. A More Intuitive Metric of Intraindustry Trade

Table 1 lists several international economics texts that report intraindustry trade data generated with a version of the **Grubel-Lloyd Index**, along with the author(s) and chapter where the indexes and associated data appear.

Table 1
International Economics Textbooks Reporting Grubel-Lloyd Intraindustry Trade Indexes

Textbook Title	Author(s)	IIT Chapter
International Economics	Sawyer and Sprinkle (2003)	Four
International Economics: Theory and Policy	Krugman and Obstfeld (2002)	Six
International Economics	Salvatore (2004)	Six
International Economics	Pugel (2003)	Five
International Economics	Husted and Melvin (2003)	Five
Windows on the World Economy	Reinert (2005)	Four
The World Economy: Trade and Finance	Yarbrough and Yarbrough (2002)	Five
World Trade and Payments	Caves, Frankel and Jones (1999)	Eight

Using the 0.00–1.00 variation of the **Grubel-Lloyd Index** and the hypothetical import/export data in columns (2) and (3) of Table 2 below, several examples of IIT index values are reported in column (4) for industries A through K. While the meaning of the extreme values (0.00 and 1.00) is straightforward, other IIT index values are non-symmetrical and therefore not subject to intuitive interpretation. To illustrate the non-symmetry of the values in Table 2, consider Industry F, whose exports are *midway* between the maximum of $100 (Industry A) and the minimum of $0 (Industry K). However, the associated IIT index is 0.67, which is not particularly intuitive. Clearly an index of 0.50 would make more sense. The other mid-range values share the same disadvantage—their values on the 0.00 to 1.00 scale are ambiguous indicators of the relative size of imports versus exports. Consequently, when interpreting intermediate values one needs to (1) remember that IIT indexes are non-symmetrical and (2) keep some "reference" values in mind, such as the index of 0.67 for the case where imports are twice exports (or vice-versa).

Table 2
Comparison: Intraindustry Trade Indexes (I) versus Intraindustry Trade Balance Proportions (P)

(1) Industry	(2) Imports (M)	(3) Exports (X)	(4) I*	(5) P*
A	$100	$100	1.00	1.00
B	$100	$ 90	0.95	0.90
C	$100	$ 80	0.89	0.80
D	$100	$ 70	0.82	0.70
E	$100	$ 60	0.75	0.60
F	$100	$ 50	0.67	0.50
G	$100	$ 40	0.57	0.40
H	$100	$ 30	0.46	0.30
I	$100	$ 20	0.33	0.20
J	$100	$ 10	0.18	0.10
K	$100	$ 0	0.00	0.00

Note: Values in boldface denote cases where imports are greater than exports.

Fortunately, the lack-of-symmetry shortcoming can be easily overcome by replacing IIT indexes with an intraindustry trade "proportion" (*P*). The proportion approach was developed by Kojima (1964) and is as follows,

$$(2) \quad P = \left(\frac{S}{G}\right),$$

where *S* is the *smaller* of imports or exports, and *G* is the *greater* of imports or exports. The intermediate *P* values in column (5) of Table 2 are not only easier to calculate than the IIT *I* entries, but are also symmetrical around Industry F. Consequently, the proportion data can be readily interpreted with each *P* value indicating the smaller of imports or exports as a proportion of the other, greater value.

Another shortcoming of both intraindustry trade indexes and proportions is that their values are the same whether imports are greater than exports or vice versa. Thus, in Table 2 if the values for exports and imports were reversed, the *I* and *P* would not change. A simple procedure for providing the reader with more information when the import/export data used to calculate *I* or *P* are not given would be to use boldface type for index values where imports exceed exports, as has been done in Table 2. Then, readers could distinguish between industries for which exports exceed imports (non-boldface entries) versus those industries where imports exceed exports (boldface entries).

Finally, with only the index or proportion values, the absolute size of trade flows is unknown. Therefore, exports of $2 million and imports of $1 million or exports of $200 million and imports of $100 million both produce an I of 0.67 or a P of 0.50. Unfortunately, this deficiency cannot be overcome without providing the import/export amounts used to generate I and P values.

3. Conclusion

The author suggests that intraindustry trade indexes be replaced with more intuitive intraindustry trade proportions and that some designation, such as bold typeface, be used to indicate cases for which imports exceed exports. These changes would (1) make the calculation process easier, (2) convey more information, and (3) provide results that are much easier to interpret.

References

Caves, R.E., J.A. Frankel and R.W. Jones (1999) *World trade and payments* (8th edition), Addison-Wesley.

Grubel, H.G. and P.J. Lloyd (1975) *Intra-industry trade: The theory and measurement of international trade in differentiated products*, John Wiley & Sons, Inc.

Husted, S. and M. Melvin (2003) *International economics* (6th edition), Addison-Wesley.

Kojima, K. (1964) "The pattern of international trade among advanced countries," *Hitotsubachi Journal of Economics* 5: 16-36.

Krugman, P.R. and M. Obstfeld (2002) *International economics: Theory and policy* (6th edition), Pearson/Addison-Wesley.

Pugel, T. (2003) *International economics* (12th edition), McGraw-Hill/Irwin.

Reinert, K.A. (2005) *Windows on the world economy*, Thomson-Southwestern.

Salvatore, D. (2004) *International economics* (8th edition), John Wiley & Sons, Inc.

Sawyer, W.C. and R.L. Sprinkle (2003) *International economics*, Prentice-Hall.

Yarbrough, B.V. and R.M. Yarbrough (2002) *The world economy: Trade and finance* (6th edition), Harcourt College Publishers.

9

Ideology in the Principles of Economics Classroom

KAMAL P. UPADHYAYA

I. Introduction

Different people define economics in different ways. However, most definitions emphasize that economics is the study of human behavior in a world of unlimited wants, but limited resources (Arnold, 2004). Alternatively, economics is sometimes defined as the study of how societies use limited resources to produce and allocate commodities among different people (Samuelson and Nordhaus, 2001). Although economics is primarily concerned with an understanding of how individuals and societies make choices given different alternatives, the study of economics includes a vast range of topics. These topics include, but are not limited to, (1) the effects of social institutions on the prices of goods/services and the factors of production, (2) the impact of fiscal and monetary policies on aggregate economic activity, (3) the analysis of trading patterns of nations and barriers to trade, (4) the analysis of exchange rate fluctuations, (5) the analysis of growth patterns among the developing countries of the world, and (6) policy recommendations regarding the distribution of income. A comprehensive list would certainly include many more topics, but the basic theme of the study of economics remains—economics provides the necessary tools to analyze and understand the production, distribution and consumption of wealth.

In the first meeting of a typical principles of economics course, a professor begins by discussing the three fundamental questions of economics: (1) what commodities are produced, and in what quantity? (2) how are the goods produced? (3) for whom are the goods produced? Clearly, in different economic "systems" these three fundamental questions are resolved in different ways. For example, in a free market economy the "market system" takes care of these questions, whereas in a "command economy" a central authority addresses these questions. In a market economy, resources are allocated based on concepts such as "efficiency," but the distribution of production is generally unequal. In a command economy, the "price system" is not allowed to coordinate production and distribution, generally resulting in mis-allocations and inefficiencies. However, production is generally thought to be distributed more evenly. Thus, economists usually face an additional dilemma—a choice between "efficiency" and "equity."

Basic economics is taught in almost all colleges/universities (including community/junior colleges) in the U.S. In most of these, one course in economics principles is a pre-requisite for completion of an undergraduate degree. In the business curriculum, at least two courses of economic principles (i.e., macro- and microeconomics) are required. Given that most upper-level business courses require a basic understanding of economic principles, in addition to the enhancement of "critical thinking skills" that usually accompanies successful completion of economics principles courses (Tobin, 1986).[1] Many of the students who enroll in economics principles courses at the college or university level have never been exposed to economics or "economic thinking" before. As such, economics instructors/professors are expected to cover all of the basic concepts, including both the *efficiency* and *equity* aspects of the discipline.[2] Unfortunately, not all economics instructors/professors set out to accomplish this mission. There are often cases wherein an economics instructor/professor covers only those aspects of the field that suits his/her ideological bias. This essay addresses the issue of teaching "ideology" in the economics principles classroom, and its impact on the future learning of students who are exposed to this particular approach in their principles courses.

2. A Standard Syllabus

Mankiw (2003) argues that students should study economics for three reasons:

- There are several phenomena in society that might spark curiosity in students. For example, why are senior citizens charged less for a movie ticket than other people? Why do the airlines charge less for a round-trip ticket if the traveler stays over Saturday night? Why is the salary of college football coaches higher than salaries of professors? Why is the standard of living different across countries? Why is it that in some countries the inflation rate is very high, while in other countries it is low/stable? Studying economics helps to understand the answers to these questions.

- Studying economics gives people to the tools to make more intelligent economic decisions. Individuals can make rational decisions about issues such as whether or not to attend graduate school or start working, or how much income to spend and how much to save. In running a business, economic literacy helps address concerns such as how much output to produce, how many workers to hire, and what price to charge. Studying economics equips students with tools that can be very helpful in their future endeavors.

- The third reason why students should study economics is because it gives them a better understanding of economic policies. For example, how will free trade affect the economy? Who bears the burden of different forms of taxation? When is economic regulation of industry warranted? What is the best way of protecting the environment? These are important policy issues. Understanding these issues makes and conscious citizen.

Given the scope of economics noted above, a typical microeconomics principles course syllabus should include the following:

Introduction:

This section usually starts with the basic definition of economics, emphasizing limited resources and unlimited desires, which leads us to make choices. Generally, it is followed by the production decisions under different economic systems, a distinction between macroeconomics and microeconomics, positive and normative economics, and the "method" of economics. In most cases, the production possibilities frontier (to point out the concept of opportunity cost and efficiency) is introduced in this section of the course. Finally, it is important that the students are familiarized with reading and using graphs before proceeding much further. Some instructors prefer to also cover specialization, trade, and the gains from free trade also in this section. Some do not cover these materials in principles classes, because they are covered later in an international economics course. Professors often suggest that the concept of the gains from trade can be explained more succinctly using the welfare analysis contained in the "market" section (see below).

Supply, Demand, and the Market:

Many professors begin this topic with the definition of a "market," using a circular flow model to help students understand the functioning of a market. Next, the law of demand and the principles behind demand curves (shifts) are often introduced, followed by these same aspects for supply. Using both the market demand and supply curves, the determination of the market price is explained to students. Often, case studies are used to explain changes in equilibrium price and quantity. It also is explained here how/why the market outcome is an *efficient* outcome. Some instructors use price control policies, such as the minimum wage and rent control laws, to demonstrate the usefulness of demand and supply concepts in explaining real life phenomena. At the end of this section of a typical economics principles course, the concept of elasticity of demand and supply (and its application) is covered.

Production and Costs:

This section covers the short-run and long-run dichotomy, the production function, the law of diminishing marginal returns, firms input choices in production, returns to scale, economic analysis of costs, and cost curves.

Market Structure and Firm Behavior:

Different market structures, such as perfect competition, monopoly, oligopoly, and monopolistic competition, are introduced in this section. This introduction is often followed by a detailed exposition of each market structure, including firm behavior in each type of environment. Instructors typically explain that perfect competition is an "ideal" environment within which resources are most *efficiently* utilized. Other market structures also are (often) compared with perfect competition to demonstrate the efficiency in the competitive model. Professors also typically describe "natural monopolies" in this section, and explain why economic regulation is often prescribed in this situation. Students also are exposed to workings of antitrust policies, implemented by governments in order to protect consumers from the market power of oligopolists.

Factor Markets:

In the *Factor Markets* section of the course, students are exposed to concepts such as how the prices of different factors of production (e.g., land, labor, capital) are determined, emphasizing the marginal productivity theory of distribution.

In addition to the topics detailed above, instructors cover additional materials depending on their interests and the availability of time.

3. Ideology in Economics

There is much disagreement among economists concerning use of the various methods of economics. Some strongly believe that economics is a positive science, which explains causes and effects. They often argue that no value judgements should be used in economic policy making. This "group" of economists generally holds a strong faith in the working of the market system, and it believes that the "invisible hand" will take care of most problems that may arise in the economy. These economists often adhere to the principles of the Austrian school. On the other end of the spectrum are those who argue that economics should be largely practiced as a normative science. While designing and implementing policies, value judgements should be given due consideration. This "group" emphasizes the equity aspects of issues of the day (over efficiency concerns). Many argue that free market systems are unfair, and some tend to rely on Marxist economics positions. Their approach to economics is often called *heterodox economics*. The University of Massachusetts at Amherst, New School University (formerly the New School for Social Research), and American University are three of the schools where this approach is emphasized in teaching, particulary in the upperclass and graduate level courses.

In any economics teaching program an Austrian economics or Marxist economics course can be offered, depending upon demand from students. In the absence of the demand for such courses, instructors sometimes integrate these economics approaches in their mainstream principles classes. In most cases, these principles courses are foundation exercises meant to provide the tools that are necessary to understand higher level courses in economics and finance. The materials covered in these two extreme approaches to microeconomics principles are presented below.

Microeconomics Principles: A Marxist Approach

Teaching with this approach often starts by indicating the virtues of capitalism and free markets. Instructors typically indicate that capitalism has improved the material standard of living of people around the world. The term *capitalism* is usually used synonymously with the phrases "free market" or "the free enterprise system." In the process of instruction, it is argued that capitalism has some major shortcomings. A typical syllabus in microeconomic theory using this approach may look like the following:

Introduction:

This section basically starts with the introduction of the capitalist economic system. It is indicated that although it is the dominant economic system at present, it should be scrutinized on the basis of what is best for society. Issues of fairness are often raised, in which it is argued that all human beings are entitled to the basic necessities in life and that they should all be treated justly and with dignity. It is typically argued that a capitalistic economic system is not capable of delivering these ends.

Surplus Production:

Here, the role of labor in production of goods and services is emphasized. It is argued that labor is the main source of production. In pure Marxism, the capitalist must pay the worker a sum that is enough to supply the worker and his family with the necessary goods for the period of hire. Under capitalism, it is argued, the worker is required to work for more hours than necessary to supply him and his family with the necessary goods, thus the capitalist is able to produce a surplus (Pearce, 1986). The role of surplus in economic growth is discussed next. The concentration of capital and formation of different classes in the society is also discussed.

Capitalism and Profit:

A capitalist's surplus is defined as a profit. Although it is recognized that the objective of the firm is to maximize its total profit, this approach to teaching economics principles points out this objective is not necessarily good for society. The classical economics idea that "the profit motive" leads to efficient outcomes, wherein production costs are minimized and consumers get the good/service at a price equal to marginal cost (and total social welfare/total economic surplus, in the traditional sense, is maximized), is de-emphasized or minimized. Instead, it is argued that business firms should not only seek profits but they should also respond to the notions of justice, fairness, and concern for others. Pure pursuit of profits, it is argued, leads to an indecent society.

Demand, Supply and Price Determination:

This approach to teaching economics principles either ignores the forces of demand and supply as the determinants of market price *or* discounts the role of the market forces of demand and supply. Some practitioners of this teaching philosophy use only demand curves to demonstrate how the price of a particular good or service is determined (see Nilsson, 2004). Instead of explaining that the forces of demand and supply come together to create an equilibrium price (quantity), instructors sometimes explain that price is simply determined by "trial and error" in the marketplace.

Market Structure:

Even though firm behavior under different market structures is typically discussed in a Marxist or heterodox course offering, the approach differs from the standard neoclassical approach. Unlike in standard microeconomics, equilibrium price and quantity are not determined by equating marginal revenue and marginal cost. Instead, price is said to include some mark-up over the average costs of production. In a competitive market, the mark-up is small due to competition, while in a monopoly the mark-up is bigger due to the presence of "market power."[3]

Labor Market:

In the heterodox approach, the labor market and the contribution of labor in the production process is covered. As pointed out earlier, it is argued that labor is the main source of production and creation of value. The labor market is often characterized as suffering from a chronic unemployment, usually as a result of the market power of employers. Therefore, within the heterodox view exploitation—paying less than what employees "deserve"—is thought to be a common feature of capitalistic societies.

In addition to the topics above, other topics, such as economic classes, the surplus theory of value, and dominance of American capitalism, also are (usually) covered in a heterodox principles course. In essence, these courses seek to demonstrate that capitalism, however it appears on its surface, ignores many "human factors."

Microeconomics Principles: A "Conservative" Approach

Neoclassical economics is the basic foundation of the conservative political-economic philosophy.[4] As such, an instructor/professor using this approach to teaching usually emphasizes how the market functions efficiently when individuals make decisions based on rational self-interests. Because individual decisions are made at the margin, marginal analysis has become a cornerstone of economics (at times microeconomic analysis is called "marginal analysis"). Instructors who use this approach believe that economics is principally a positive science, and that there is usually little role for government intervention in the economy. It is typically thought that government policies that affect individual decision-making are nothing less than an intrusion on individual rights. Those on the extreme—Austrian economists—even argue that public goods such as national defense, the judiciary and even the currency, can be provided by the private sector. Because of their strong ideological feelings for low levels of government involvement in an individual's daily activities, their course instruction may focus on demonstrating the faults of government policies rather than the teaching of the tools of economic theory, that students generally need to grasp upper level courses in economics, finance and business. Unlike standard or traditional neoclassical economics, Austrian economics does not rely (principally) on the *scientific method*.

Topics typically covered on a microeconomics principles syllabus using this approach include:

Introduction:

This section usually begins with a definition of economics as "the study of the use of limited resources that have alternative uses." Instructors generally explain what is meant by scarcity. This is followed by the explanation that resources have alternative uses, therefore individuals and societies must make choices. It is also typically mentioned that an abundance of resources does not make a country wealthy. Instead, an economic system in which resources are used efficiently leads to a higher national income. It is also mentioned that in a free market system, individuals are free to make choices, and as a result resources are better utilized than in a socialist (or other) system wherein governments make most, if not all, decisions. Before concluding this section, it is usually stated that the price system is at the heart of a free market economy. Prices coordinate production and consumption in the economy, and efficient resource use/allocation occurs through the price mechanism.

Prices and Markets:

This section begins with the introduction of the concept of opportunity costs, and it is often explained that from the standpoint of society that the cost of something is the value of the resources that went into producing have in alternative uses. That cost is reflected in the market price (Sowell, 2004: 10-11). With examples from different countries, it is also explained that in countries where the price system is allowed to function freely (i.e., without much government intervention), economies grow much faster than in those where the economies are not allowed to operate freely (due to government intervention). This is often followed with discussion on price controls (i.e., price ceilings and price floors) and why such policies fail. Instructors also often discuss the political economy of price control policies, with examples from agriculture, rent controls, and minimum wage laws.

Industry and Commerce:

In lieu of a standard or traditional microeconomic approach to market structures, instructors who employ this approach to teaching economics principles often begin this section with discussion about how "big businesses" emerge. The competitive nature, it is typically stated, of the market forces businesses to continuously adjust their strategies, making them more efficient, while consumers are more satisfied from better products/services that emerge from this "competitive" process. It is explained that the objective of the business firm is to maximize profits. As such, businesses seek to use the most efficient method of production, often leading to a larger scale of production. It is also explained that under socialism, wherein the importance of profits is minimized, most of the production and distribution are done by the government, either directly or through regulations. In either case, efficiency is lost. Antitrust laws and economic regulations are discussed in relation to the market power of monopolies and oligopolies, but it is typically stated that the regulatory agencies are either not capable of regulating business firms or that they regulate in the interests of the business firms (i.e., the "capture theory" of regulation). Most of the discussion in this section is done with minimal assistance from the traditional production and cost curves.

Labor Market:

Unlike in a traditional principles course, this topic does not focus heavily on how wage rates are determined. Instead, focus is placed on how the labor market is controlled and distorted by politicians and labor unions. The pitfalls of job security legislation, minimum wage laws, labor unions/collective bargaining are mainly discussed in this part of the course.

International Trade and Immigration:

Because conservative economists believe in the free market (enterprise) system, they typically have a strong faith in free international trade. Therefore, much of this section is devoted to covering the issue of free trade (and immigration). In addition to covering the basic reasons why nations engage in trade, major myths about international trade and immigration are also discussed.

A cursory look at the above discussion shows that the conservative approach to economics is consistent with traditional treatment to some degree. But, a problem lies with the focus of the instructor. Instead of covering the tools of economics and their application to real world problems, instructors using this approach often spend significant time discussing the ills of government intervention without the assistance of basic economics tools. As such, students remain ill-equipped to learn in upper level classes related to economics.

The extreme of this philosophy is Austrian economics. Though the Austrians adhere to the principles of the market system, they do not typically employ the neo-classical approach to economics subjects. Because Austrians believe in *methodological individualism* and *subjectivism*, they do not rely on the mathematical, statistical or graphical methods that are presented/used in traditional microeconomics principles texts (Walker, 2004). As a result, their students are often not well-exposed to the tools they will need to use along the future path of their academic careers.

4. Concluding Comments

Principles of economics courses equip students with the necessary tools for understanding upper-level courses in economics, finance, and general business. For students not majoring in a business, or related, discipline, economics helps him/her develop critical thinking skills. For these reasons, it is important to cover the core materials/tools when teaching economics principles. Instead, instructors sometimes shape their principles syllabus to fit a particular ideology. While doing so, they either do not cover the core materials/tools, or they do not have enough time in the academic semester to cover the core materials/tools thoroughly. As a result, students may move on to upper-level course ill-equipped to understand the topics covered in them. Instructors should take care to cover mainstream economics tools and concepts in principles courses, and perhaps add elective courses covering particular ideological elements to the economics curriculum.

Notes

* The author thanks Armando Rodriguez and participants in the Brown Bag Seminar Series at the University of New Haven for helpful comments and suggestions.

1. Nieswiadomy (1998) reports that economics majors perform among the top three disciplines on the LSAT. Many attribute this lofty ranking to the advanced reasoning skills of economics students.

2. Stated differently, economics teachers are often expected to cover both the *positive* and *normative* aspects of economics (see Heath, 1994, for an excellent discussion of the distinction between the *positive* and *normative* branches of economics).

3. The heterodox view often merges the concepts of "competition" and "monopolistic competition" that are found (separately) in the neoclassical or traditional micro-course.

4. See Walker (2004) for a more thorough presentation of the topics covered in this approach.

References

Arnold, R.A. (2004) *Economics* (6th edition), Mason, OH: Thomson-Southwestern.

Heath, W.C. (1994) "Value judgements and the principles of economics textbook," *Southern Economic Journal* 60: 1,060-1,064.

Mankiw, N.G. (2003) *Principles of economics* (3rd edition), New York, NY: Southwestern College Publishing.

Nieswiadomy, M. (1998) "LSAT scores of economics majors," *Journal of Economic Education* 29: 377-379.

Nilsson, E. (2004) *Capitalism, power, profits, and human flourishing,* economics.csub.edu (visit faculty/nilsson/courses/econ200/Introductory_Macroeconomics).

Pearce, D.W. [ed.] (1986) *MIT dictionary of modern economics*, Cambridge, MA: The MIT Press.

Samuelson, P.A. and W.D. Nordhaus (2001) *Economics* (17th edition), New York, NY: Irwin/McGraw-Hill.

Sowell, T. (2004) *Basic economics: A citizen's guide to the economy*, New York, NY: Basic Books.

Tobin, J. (1986) "Economic literacy isn't marginal investment," *The Wall Street Journal* (July 9th).

Walker, D.L. (2004) "Austrian economics," *A concise encyclopedia of economics*, econlib.org.

10

Bracketology 101
Using Sports to Apply Probabilistic Concepts from Elementary Econometrics

FRANKLIN G. MIXON, JR. AND MICHAEL C. WITHERS

I. Introduction

The application of economics to sports is growing by leaps and bounds in the academic literature. Its importance can be seen with the recent introduction of a new periodical dedicated to the subject—*The Economics of Sports*—as well as the recent publication of two textbooks devoted entirely to the subject (Fort, 2003; Leeds and von Allmen, 2005). Since 1990, empirical work in the area of sports economics has become so common it has spawned a new economics term, "sportometrics," following the title of a now well-known edited volume by Fleisher, Goff and Tollison (1990).

It is certainly no secret to many economics educators that the use of sports-related topics can motivate and enhance the study of economics in general, and econometrics in particular (see Schwertman, McCready and Howard, 1991). As Schwertman *et al.* (1991: 35) indicate, "[a]thletics in general and postseason competition in particular afford such opportunities to demonstrate, in the class-room, the application of probabilistic concepts." Taking a cue from Schwertman *et al.* (1991), this essay uses results from the NCAA Men's Basketball Tournament (over the period 1985-2004) to illustrate the application of probability concepts in economics and econometrics. While the literature on statistical probabilities is replete with interesting case studies (see Anderson, Jackson, and Steagall, 1994; Shachar and Nalebuff, 1999), this particular athletic event offers a compelling example given that a significant portion of the U.S. population engages in "office betting pools" to predict the tournament winner each April. Interest in the tournament is so great that Americans have come to recognize the annual spectacle as "March Madness," and television networks such as CBS and ESPN devote a significant amount of coverage to expert analyses of the individual contests that make up the tournament's bracket (these analyses are often referred to as "bracketology"). Our aim is to illustrate the applicability of probability estimates obtained from limited dependent variables models to topics of interest to students in statistics and elementary econometrics. In doing so, our results can then be compared to those from models that do not include regression-based analysis.

2. Bringing "March Madness" to the Classroom

Each March brings much of America's attention to what is often referred to as one of the greatest of all sports spectacles—the annual NCAA Men's Basketball Championship Tournament.[1] The excitement begins with the tournament committee's Selection (of teams) Shows, which are traditionally aired on CBS and ESPN. The "top 64" teams in the nation are seeded (from 1 through 64) by a committee of conference commissioners, former coaches, and other college basketball "experts."[2] The committee's seedings are then dissected by college basketball's television personalities, such as Dick Vitale, Digger Phelps and Jay Bilas of ESPN, and by Billy Packer and Clark Kellogg of CBS.[3] In recent years, the analyses of these so-called experts has come to be known as "bracketology."[4]

On the Monday following "Selection Show Sunday" most national newspapers provide extensive coverage of the tournament field. Many include a full-page scan of the tournament bracket that fans can use to mark their predictions. These predictions have become popularized through informal "office betting pools" around the country, and such pools have spawned these and other types of prediction "contests" that are now prevalent in college dorms and fraternities/sororities, on the Internet, in local sports bars/pubs, and in local/national newspapers. The popularity of these types of "pools" and "contests" suggests that the March Madness phenomenon might serve as a compelling and interesting tool for applying probability concepts in econometrics and statistics courses.

This essay provides instructors with a template for incorporating this great sports spectacle into an elementary econometrics or statistics discussion. To do so, we gathered results from the universe of NCAA tournaments since the adoption of the 64-team format (i.e., 1985). Our data set includes results from the most recent tournament in March/April of 2004. The tournament is divided into four separate regionals, with 16 teams in each.[5] The 16 teams in each regional are seeded (ranked) based on team strength, from one (the strongest team) through 16 (the weakest team). Most analysts view the NCAA Tournament construct as having four separate tournaments—the Regionals—where four champions emerge to face each other in what is known as "The Final Four."[6] For this study, the unit of observation is the result of each NCAA Regional Tournament (hereafter NRT) game over the 20-year time span from 1985-2004. Thus, we have a relatively large data set (i.e., n=1,200) and a potentially rich source of information with which to examine winning/losing probabilities in college basketball.

Our model is presented in (1) below,

(1) hiwin* = $X\beta + \varepsilon$,

where hiwin* represents the tendency of higher seeded teams to win a given NRT game, X is a vector of exogenous variables that impact hiwin*, β is a vector of parameters to be estimated, and ε is a random error term.[7] The higher seeded team's *tendency* to win a given NRT game (i.e., hiwin*) is assumed to be a continuous, latent variable. What is observed, however, is the outcome of a given NRT game, which is referred to as hiwin, a dichotomous variable equal to 1 for games won by the higher seeded team, and 0 otherwise. If ε is assumed to follow the logistic distribution, then the probability that the higher seeded team wins a given NRT game is given by the familiar logit formula in (2) below (Kennedy, 2003; Greene, 2003; Hill, Griffiths and Judge, 2001):

(2) $P(\text{hiwin}=1) = [e^{X\beta}/(1 + e^{X\beta})]$.

Because our essay serves as a template for econometrics and statistics instructors, our model for predicting winning probabilities is fairly parsimonious, making use of three exogenous variables. Definitions for each of the three regressors contained in X (i.e., seeddiff, hiseed, and roundone) are presented in Table 1 (along with hiwin).[8] Over the 20 years that the NCAA has followed the current format (excluding the new play-in game), about 72 percent of all NRT games have been won by the higher seeded team. The average absolute difference in the seeds of teams over the 1,200 NRT games since 1985 is about 6.5 seeding places (see seeddiff), while the average seeding for the highest seeded team in these same 1,200 games is about 3.5 (on a 1 to 16 scale). Lastly, given the single elimination format of the NRT, slightly more than half of all NRT games have been "Round 1" games (each NRT has four rounds).

Table 1
Variable Definitions and Summary Statistics

Variable	Definition	Mean	Std. Deviation
hiwin	Dummy variable equal to one for NRT games won by the higher seeded team, and zero otherwise.	0.7233	0.4475
seeddiff	The absolute value of the difference in seedings between two given NRT opponents.	6.5517	4.1700
hiseed	The seeding of the "higher seeded" team between two given NRT opponents.	3.5933	2.3422
roundone	Dummy variable equal to one for first round games in a given NRT, and zero otherwise.	0.5333	0.4991

Note: The data were collected by the authors from ncaa.org, the official website of the NCAA.

One expects that the larger the absolute difference in the seeds of the two teams in a given game, the greater the probability that the higher seeded team wins the particular game. Given the vagaries of seeding teams beyond the top four or five in any given NRT—even with the use of so-called experts in the seeding process—one would expect that the higher the seed held by the highest seeded team in an NRT game the greater the probability that the highest seeded team wins the game (see endnote 7). Thus, we expect that hiseed will be negatively related to $P(\text{hiwin}=1)$. Finally, the roundone dummy is included to capture any "higher seed advantage" built into the NRT format; such an advantage would exist mainly in the first round of the NRT, and would be indicated by a positive relationship between roundone and $P(\text{hiwin}=1)$.

Results from a logit specification of (1) using hiwin are presented below in (3). The Model χ^2 statistic indicates that the three regressors are jointly significant in

$$(3) \quad \text{hiwin} = 0.1368 + 0.1769\text{seeddiff} - 0.0598\text{hiseed} + 0.0489\text{roundone}$$
$$(0.61) \qquad\quad (6.95) \qquad\qquad (-1.39) \qquad\qquad (0.24)$$
$$n=1,200 \text{ Model } \chi^2=125.74$$

explaining the probability that the higher seeded team wins a given NRT contest. Above, seeddiff is significantly related to hiwin (as indicated by the t-values in parentheses). Marginal probability estimates for the first two parameters are 0.035 and -0.012, respectively (see Caudill and Jackson, 1989). The marginal probability associated with seeddiff suggests that a small increase in seeddiff leads to about a 3.5 percentage point increase in the probability that the higher seeded team wins any NRT game, *ceteris paribus*. Total probabilities computed using (2) and (3) above are reported below, and they are compared to non-regression based probabilities reported earlier in Schwertman *et al.* (1991).

3. Probability Estimates and Goodness-of-Fit Tests

Calculating the probability of any team winning the NRT requires the evaluation of the probability for each game played (using equations (2) and (3)). To compute the probability of each of the teams eventually winning the NRT, it is necessary to make the same simplifying assumption that is usually made in the literature—that the games are independent (see Schwertman, *et al.*, 1991: 36). As Schwertman *et al.* (1991: 36) indicate,

> "Intangible effects that can affect the independence of each game are very dif-
> ficult to measure...Although the independence assumtpion may alter the
> exact probabilities somewhat, we nevertheless still have useful models that
> should provide a reasonable approximation to the actual probabilities as well
> as a practical and interesting probability exercise."

Given that the purpose of our essay is to provide interesting applications of regression-based probabilistic concepts, it seems reasonable to follow the advice of Schwertman *et al.* (1991) here as well.

Applying the results in equation (3) above to equation (2), we find that the probability that a top-seeded team wins a given NRT is about 0.280. This figure falls inside, but near the lower end, of a range of probabilities from a non-regression based approach in Scwhertman *et al.* (1991). Their estimates range from 0.275 to 0.519. These figures are all presented in Table 2. For comparison, we also computed the probability of a top-seeded team winning a given NRT using a linear probability model (hereafter LPM), and obtained a probability estimate of about 0.288.[9] Our logit (LPM) estimate of the probability that a number two-seeded teams wins a given NRT is about 0.156 (0.155). This figure is slightly below the low end of the range produced by the non-regression based equations in Schwertmann *et al.* (1991). Their estimates range from 0.188 to 0.216 (see Table 2). Finally, our logit (LPM) estimate of the probability that a number three-seeded team is victorious in a given NRT is about 0.097 (0.089). Again, this estimate falls just below the low end of the range of estimates in Schwertman *et al.* (1991) that runs from 0.107 to 0.154.[10]

Table 2
Logistic and LPM Probabilities of Winning the NCAA Regional Basketball Tournament

Seed Position	Logit Model	LPM Model	*Schwertman et al., 1991*		
			(1)	(2)	(3)
1	0.28000	0.28814	0.51922	0.27477	0.45883
2	0.15562	0.15526	0.21604	0.20834	0.18813
3	0.09672	0.08886	0.10679	0.15429	0.11032

Following Schwertman *et al.* (1991), an examination of how well our estimates predict actual outcomes can be performed using a traditional chi-squared test (see Anderson, Sweeney and Williams, 1996). To do so, we compared the results from the 24 NRTs during the period 1985-1990, the period examined by Schwertman *et al.* (1991), to the results predicted by our logit model (LPM) for each of the top three seeding positions. These tests are presented in Table 3, along with those from Schwertman *et al.* (1991). As Table 3 indicates, 18 of the 24 NRTs during the 1985-1990 period were won by the top three seeded teams (10, five and three, respectively). The outcome predicted by each of the three

Table 3
Goodness-of-Fit Analysis

Group (seed #)	Observed	Logit Model	LPM Model	*Schwertman et al., 1991*		
				(1)	(2)	(3)
1	10	6.720	6.915	12.461	6.595	11.012
2	5	3.735	3.726	5.185	5.000	4.515
3	3	2.321	2.133	2.563	3.703	2.648
4-16	6	11.224	11.226	3.791	8.702	5.825
		$\chi^2_{(3)} = 4.659$	$\chi^2_{(3)} = 4.597$	$\chi^2_{(3)} = 1.855$	$\chi^2_{(3)} = 2.731$	$\chi^2_{(3)} = 0.197$
	p-values	0.199	0.204	0.603	0.435	0.978

Note: The expectations for our models (logit and LPM) for seeds 4 through 16 are equal to 24 minus the expectations for seeds 1 through 3. For the χ^2 statistics, the numbers in parentheses represent degrees of freedom.

Schwertman *et al.* (1991) methods is not statistically different from the actual pattern of success during the study period. In two of these three models (cases (1) and (3) above in Table 3), the predicted values were very compatible with the empirical data. Model (2) above produces a different result, though the chi-squared test also failed to reject it as being unsuitable even well beyond the customary significance levels.

Our logit model produces a series of expected outcomes that test most like model (2) from Schwertman *et al.* (1991). The logit result is supported by the LPM finding, again producing a chi-squared statistic near 4.6, below that required for usual levels of significance.[11] Thus, neither set of models appears to suffer from oversimplification in its use of independence (as explained above), and our regression-based approach provides a suitable (alternative) method for examining outcomes in the NCAA Men's Basketball Tournament over time. Below, we explore common practices in NCAA "bracketology" that will be familiar to students who participate in "March Madness" prediction pools.

4. More Regression-Based Bracketology

Participants in office- and school-based bracket pools (betting pools) range from individuals who watch a large portion of televised college basketball action from November through February to those whose knowledge about college basketball comes only from what they gather from casual conversation. A common practice among people across the whole spectrum of bracket pool participants is to "predict" that the top four seeds in each regional will advance on to round two of each NRT. According to our logit model (LPM), the probability of complete success in a given NRT following this "rule" is 0.621 (0.630) (see row four of Table 4 below). The probability of having the four top seeds advance to round two in all four NRTs—which is equivalent to having the top 16 seeds in the entire NCAA tournament field advance to round two—is only 0.148 (0.158) using the logit model (LPM) estimates (see row five of Table 4).

The probability that the top half of a NRT bracket advances to round two (i.e., the top eight seeds advance to round two) falls to 0.085 (0.085) using the logit model (LPM) estimates (see row two of Table 4). The probability of having this occur in all four NRTs—which is equivalent to having the top 32 seeds (i.e., the top half of all seeds) in the entire NCAA Tournament field advance to round two—is only 0.00005 using either the logit model or LPM. This type of prediction is a common practice among amateur prognosticators.

A vast majority of amateur prognosticators place the four top-seeded teams in the Final Four of the entire tournament. Again, this is equivalent to suggesting that the top NRT seed wins each NRT. As Table 2 indicates, our models predict that the probability of a top-seeded team winning a given NRT ranges from only 0.28 to 0.29. Schwertman *et al.* (1991) predict a somewhat better outlook of 0.27 to 0.52. However, considering that there are four NRTs in each NCAA Championship Tournament, the probability of observing four number one seeds

Table 4
Some Additional Probability Estimates

	Logit Model	LPM Model	Schwertman et al., 1991		
			(1)	(2)	(3)
Four #1 Seeds Advance to Final 4	0.00615	0.00689	0.07268	0.00570	0.04432
Seeds 1-8 Advance Past First Round of an NRT Bracket	0.08502	0.08458			
Seeds 1-32 Advance Past First Round of a Tournament Bracket	0.00005	0.00005			
Seeds 1-4 Advance Past First Round of an NRT Bracket	0.62073	0.63014			
Seeds 1-16 Advance Past First Round of a Tournament Bracket	0.14846	0.15767			
"Perfect Progression" in an NRT Bracket	0.00306	0.00338			
"Perfect Progression" in all NRT brackets	0.088e-9	0.131e-9			

Note: The probabilities listed above for Schwertman *et al.* (1991) are computed by the authors using the probability estimates they present in their article.

advancing into the Tournament's Final Four ranges from only 0.006 to 0.007 using the logit/LPM approaches here, and from 0.006 to 0.073 using the non-regression based approaches in Schwertman *et al.* (1991). These probabilities are all presented in row one of Table 4.[12]

Another common practice among amateur pool participants is to predict a "perfect progression" in a particular NRT. Madsen (1991) examined the probability of a perfect progression in college football (see Table 5 for an example of a perfect progression—the 1988 Big Eight Conference Football Standings). Specifically, he analyzed the probability that a perfect mathematical progression of any permutation would occur in the end-of-season standings (during 1988) in the Big Eight Conference. Madsen estimates that the probability of a perfect progression of any permutation in the Big Eight Conference ranges from 0.0038

Table 5
An Example of "Perfect Progression": The 1988 Big 8 Conference Football Standings

Team	Big 8 Conference Record	
	Wins	Losses
Nebraska Cornhuskers	7	0
Oklahoma Sooners	6	1
Oklahoma State Cowboys	5	2
Colorado Buffaloes	4	3
Iowa State Cyclones	3	4
Missouri Tigers	2	5
Kansas Jayhawks	1	6
Kansas State Wildcats	0	7

Source: Madsen (1991).

to 0.1448, depending on the length of the history that is used to estimate relative frequencies (of outcomes).

In the context of a given NRT, a "perfect progression" implies that the higher seeded team wins each contest in the NRT. Again, assuming independence, our logit model (LPM) predicts that the probability of perfect progression is approximately 0.0031 (0.0034). Using Madsen's illustration approach, this equates to one perfect progression in every 323 (294) NRTs. With four NRTs played each year (or each NCAA Tournament), that reduces to one perfect progression in every 81 (74) years. Of course, if one estimates the probability of a perfect progression for all four regionals in a tournament, the results are much smaller (see Table 4). Our logit model (LPM) produces an estimate of the probability of a "perfect" set of (four) NRTs of 0.088e-9 (0.131e-9). This equates to one perfect set of (four) NRTs in every 11.1 billion (7.7 billion) tournaments.

5. The UConn Huskies, 2004 Bracketology, and Conclusions

In 2004, the Connecticut Huskies won the NCAA Men's Basketball Championship. It was their second national championship in men's basketball in less than a decade. The Huskies' road to the Final Four was paved through the Phoenix (AZ) Regional, where they were seeded second. As Table 2 above suggests, the probability that the Huskies would win the Phoenix NRT, as a number two seed, stood at about 0.16 (0.20) going in, using our (the Schwertman *et al.*) models. The Huskies ultimately defeated Vermont (#15), DePaul (#7), Vanderbilt (#6), and Alabama (#8) to win the Phoenix NRT. The *a priori* probability of accomplishing such a feat, using our logit model, was about 0.327, or one in three tries. This is just over twice as large as the probability of successfully navigating through the toughest (*a priori*) string of teams possible, which would have been Vermont (#15), DePaul (#7), North Carolina State (#3), and Stanford (#1). At the same time, this figure (0.327) is just over one-half the probability of vanquishing the easiest (*a priori*) schedule of opponents possible for the 2004 Phoenix Regional, which was Vermont (#15), Dayton (#10), Louisiana–Lafayette (#14), and Texas–San Antonio (#16). The (estimated) probability of Connecticut succeeding against this latter string of teams falls slightly above 0.6 (or three in five) using our model. Of course, none of these estimates factors in the odds of going further to beat Duke (#1, Atlanta Regional) and then Georgia Tech (#3, St. Louis Regional) for the 2004 NCAA Championship.

Predicting outcomes in a given NRT is a difficult task. Many bracket pools employ a system wherein the entire set of results is predicted before the first game is played, which means that early "mistakes" are usually compounded. The only things that are *certain* about "March Madness" prognosticating are that (1) the number one seed will always defeat the sixteenth seed in round one of each NRT, and (2) the whole spectacle provides an interesting avenue for applying probabilistic concepts in elementary econometrics classroom discussions. Perhaps referring to (1) above as a "certainty" is a bit too strong. There have been 80 NRTs since the new 64-team format was adopted in 1985, and not a single 16-seed has ever knocked off a top seeded team in the opening round. What is the probability of that streak occurring? The answer, 0.0084. It appears as though item number one in our two-item list of *certainties* above is just about due for removal (within the next ten years?). Maybe this and other facets of the tournament would make good material for Bracketology 102.

Notes

* We thank the NCAA for making the tournament results data available to us. Any errors are our own.

1. The NCAA Men's Basketball Championship Tournament traditionally begins near the middle of March each year, and usually runs through the early part of April. The fan hysteria surrounding the event is often referred to as "March Madness." The tournament is so popular in the U.S. that many U.S. corporations (e.g., Ford, Pizza Hut) gear much of their March/April advertising effort to its fans by incorporating the "March Madness" theme in commercial ads.

2. The Tournament Selection Committee chooses 65 teams for the tournament field. The two teams seeded 64 and 65 face each other in a "play in" game about two or three nights before the "traditional" tournament begins. The winner of this game is seeded 64 within the "final" field of 64 teams. Conference champions generally receive automatic bids, while several other top schools receive "at-large" bids as a reward for a "successful" season of play. The Selection Committee offers at-large bids as a function of winning percentage, schedule difficulty, timing of peak performance, and other attributes. The Selection Shows on CBS and ESPN air in the late afternoon of the "Selection Day," which is traditionally held on an early Sunday in March.

3. Many of college basketball's television personalities are "household names" (e.g., Dick Vitale), given the popularity of the sport and its Championship Tournament in the United States. Their analyses of the Selection Committee's product are presented on the Selection Sunday shows, and coaches whose teams were "on the bubble" (i.e., at the margin for consideration) but were left out are often invited to give on-air (live) interviews. These exchanges are often heated, given the importance of tournament participation to a program's revenues and visibility (see Fort, 2003 and Leeds and von Allmen, 2005 for discussion of revenue sources to schools in the NCAA).

4. Use of the term plays on the notion that such expert analyses are "scientific."

5. The regionals have historically been named after sections of the country (e.g., South, East, West, Mideast, etc.). Today, the four regionals are named after their host cities. In 2004, these were East Rutherford (NJ), Phoenix, Atlanta and St. Louis.

6. In fact, much of the prestige tournament participants are vying for is achieved upon reaching "The Final Four" (i.e., winning one of the Regional tournaments).

7. As indicated above, NRT seeding follows a format wherein the strongest team is seeded (ranked) #1, and the weakest team is seeded (ranked) #16. In NCAA Tournament terminology, #1 is the "highest" seeding, while #16 is the "lowest" seeding. Given NRT seeding and pairing (bracketing), the seeding difference between teams in a given NRT game ranges from one to 15 (in absolute value).

8. Boulier and Stekler (1999), Caudill and Godwin (2002), and Caudill (2003) have used similar models to explore the usefulness of seedings as a predictor of the outcome of individual games in the tournament. Our model will be used (later in this chapter) to explore the probabilities associated with various tournament outcomes, such as those contemplated by "betting pool" participants.

9. Computation of the LPM estimate might be useful for instructors, given problems that are sometimes encountered in obtaining logit estimates when observation-specific and/or group dummies are present in the model (see Caudill, 1987 and 1988).

10. Though our essay concentrates on the top three seeds, it is simply a template for bringing this type of analysis into a classroom discussion of probability estimates obtained from regression.

11. We are aware of the limitations of the chi-square goodness-of-fit test when values for the expected outcomes fall below five (see Sweeney *et al.*, 1996: 426-428). Our use of it follows Schwertman *et al.* (1991), and allows for a comparison between the two methods of obtaining predicted probabilities in the NCAA Tournament (i.e., nonregression-based and regression-based methods).

12. Once again our results, using logit and LPM, closely track those of Model 2 in Schwertman *et al.* (1991).

References

Anderson, D.R., D.J. Sweeney and T.A. Williams (1996) *Statistics for business and economics*, Minneapolis/St. Paul, MN: West Publishing Company.

Anderson, S.C., J.D. Jackson, and J.W. Steagall (1994) "A note on odds in the cattle futures market," *Journal of Economics and Finance* 18: 357-365.

Boulier, B.L. and H.O. Stekler (1999) "Are sports seedings good predictors?" *International Journal of Forecasting* 15: 83-91.

Caudill, S.B. (1987) "Dichotomous choice models and dummy variables," *The Statistician* 36: 381-383.

——————— (1988) "An advantage of linear probability models over probit or logit," *Oxford Bulletin of Economics and Statistics* 50: 425-427.

——————— (2003) "Predicting discrete outcomes with the maximum score estimator: The case of the NCAA men's basketball tournament," *International Journal of Forecasting* 19: 313-317.

——————— and N.H. Godwin (2002) "Heterogeneous skewness in binary choice models: Predicting outcomes in the men's NCAA basketball tournament," *Journal of Applied Statistics* 29: 991-1,001.

——————— and J.D. Jackson (1989) "Measuring marginal effects in limited-dependent variable models," *The Statistician* 38: 203-206.

Fort, R.D. (2003) *Sports economics*, Upper Saddle River, NJ: Prentice Hall.

Goff, B.L. and R.D. Tollison (1990) *Sportometrics*, College Station, TX: Texas A&M University Press.

Greene, W.H. (2003) *Econometric analysis*, Upper Saddle River, NJ: Prentice Hall.

Hill, R.C., W.E. Griffiths, and G.G. Judge (2001) *Undergraduate econometrics*, New York, NY: John Wiley & Sons, Inc.

Kennedy, P. (2003) *A guide to econometrics*, Cambridge, MA: The MIT Press.

Leeds, M. A. and P. von Allmen (2005) *The economics of sports*, Reading, MA: Addison-Wesley.

Madsen, R, (1991) "On the probability of a perfect progression," *The American Statistician* 45: 214-216.

Schwertman, N.C., T.A. McCready, and L. Howard (1991) "Probability models for the NCAA regional basketball tournaments," *The American Statistician* 45: 35-38.

Shachar, R. and B. Nalebuff (1999) "Follow the leader: Theory and evidence on political participation," *American Economic Review* 89: 525-547.

Part III.

*The Sociology of
Economic Education*

11

Ranking Institutions Based on Economic Education Scholarship

MELODY LO AND M.C. SUNNY WONG

I. Introduction

Research productivity is often viewed as the measure of success among higher education institutions. Some studies rank U.S./international economics departments based on the faculty's research productivity (Dusansky and Vernon, 1998; Lalaitzidakis et al., 2003). They estimate the ranking by measuring how many articles each school has published in the top-ranking journals and how many times the published articles have been cited in the literature. Instead of measuring research productivity of the faculty in each department, Laband (1986) ranks each department based on the productivity of its Ph.D. graduates. These studies measure success solely in terms of *research quality*. This paper constructs a new ranking of economics departments worldwide according to a measure of *teaching quality*. We use the research contribution to economic education literature as a proxy for teaching quality (in economics). Much of the research in economic education is related to the effectiveness and innovations in economic teaching. As such, we assume that schools with greater contributions to the economic education literature have a comparative advantage in teaching economics.

Among the (few) journals in the field of economic education, we select the top field journal, the *Journal of Economic Education* (*JEE*), as the standard measure of teaching-related research productivity with which to rank institutions worldwide. This information is potentially useful to students seeking to be economics majors. Our ranking may also provide a normative argument for schools to real-locate their resources toward teaching and research more appropriately.

2. Data and Methodology

Teaching-based research productivity is evaluated by the number of articles and the number of pages published in the *Journal of Economic Education*. We collected more than 950 articles published in 114 issues of the *JEE* starting from the first issue in 1969 and ending with the third issue of the thirty fifth volume in 2004. Because we are only interested in teaching-related research output among higher education institutions, we excluded non-teaching organizations in the private and government sectors from our data set.[1] In all, our data set includes 416 institutions that have published articles in the *JEE* during the sample period.

Our first measure is the number of articles published, based on institutional affiliations for the authors. For coauthorships, each institution represented is credited with one publication only, regardless of the number of times a particular institution appears in a string of authors. However, we note that, for example, one publication with three coauthors is very different from three single-authored publications. Therefore, we measure individual productivity according to the number of pages in each article. For a paper published by n coauthors, we assume proportional production by each author, such that each author is credited with $1/n$ of the total pages in the article.

3. Results

Table 1 presents the ranking of institutions (worldwide) based on the number of articles published between 1969 and 2004. To conserve space, we report the Top 100 institutions in the table.[2] We found that the institutions that have con-tributed the most to economic education research are Vanderbilt University, University of Nebraska, Purdue University, Indiana University, University of Illinois, Illinois State University, University of Wisconsin, University of Georgia, Denison University, Stanford University and Princeton University. Educators affiliated with these schools published a total of 235 articles in the *JEE* during the sample period. Relatively speaking, these top schools published about 20 percent of the articles in the journal during the period under study. Moreover, we see that some schools with well-established reputations, such as Harvard University, Massachusetts Institute of Technology and the University of California at Berkeley contribute relatively less to the economic education literature. On the other, we find that some liberal arts colleges and Master's degree-granting colleges/universities are ranked near the top of the list (see Table 1).[3] For example, Denison University, a liberals arts university, is ranked in the Top 10, while James Madison University and California State University at Hayward, both Master's degree-granting (only) institutions, rank in the 15th and 20th place, respectively. These positions indicate that teaching-oriented schools are more concerned with the effectiveness of, and innovations in, economics teaching/instruction. This approach is beneficial to students majoring in economics (and others) at the undergraduate level.

As pointed out above, measuring the weighted share of publications might be more a accurate indication of how schools contribute to the literature in economic education. Table 2 shows the ranking of institutions according to the adjusted pages of articles published in the *JEE*. The first column of Table 2 indicates the ranking of each school during the sample period, 1969-2004. Not surprisingly, schools that published more articles tend to have more adjusted pages in the journal. We note that most of the top schools in Table 1 remain at the top when using the adjusted pages method. Using Figure 1, we also note that the Top 50 institutions (out of 416) have contributed about 50 percent of the adjusted pages in the *JEE* since 1969.

Table 1
Ranking of Institutions Based on the Number of Articles Published in the *Journal of Economic Education*

School	Total Publications	Rank	School	Total Publications	Rank
Vanderbilt U	37	1	S IL U, Edwardsville	5	
U of Nebraska, Lincoln	35	2	Syracuse U	5	
Purdue U	31	3	Texas Tech U	5	
Indiana U, Bloomington	25	4	U of Missouri, Rolla	5	
U of IL, Urbana-Champ	22	5	U of Nebraska, Omaha	5	
IL State U	20	6	U of Notre Dame	5	
U of WI, Madison	16	7	U of Pittsburgh	5	
U of Georgia, Athens	14	8	Western IL U	5	
Denison U	13	9	Berry College	4	55
Stanford U	13		Georgia State U	4	
Princeton U	13		Hamilton College	4	
Miami U (OH)	11	12	Holy Cross College	4	
Mississippi State U	11		Kansas State U	4	
U of MN, Twin Cities	11		Murray State U	4	
NYU	11		Ohio State U	4	
Duke U	10	16	Oklahoma State U	4	

James Madison U	10		Pacific Lutheran U	4	
U of Delaware	10		Pennsylvania State U	4	
U of NC, Chapel Hill	10		Pomona College	4	
Auburn U	9	20	Towson State U	4	
CA St. U, Hayward	9		Trinity U	4	
U of Missouri, Columbia	9		U of Cincinnati	4	
Ball State U	8	23	U of Iowa	4	
Clemson U	8		U of Chicago	4	
John Carroll U	8		U of Central FL	4	
Northern IL U	8		U of Melbourne	4	
U of CO, Boulder	8		U of MN, Minneapolis	4	
U of WI, Milwaukee	8		U of NC, Asheville	4	
Bradley U	7	29	U of North Dakota	4	
Harvard U	7		U of Richmond	4	
MIT	7		U of South Carolina	4	
U of WI, Lacrosse	7		U of SW Louisiana	4	
U of CA, Berkeley	7		U of Virginia	4	
Weber State U	7		UCLA	4	
Wellesley College	7		Utah State U	4	
Mary Washington Coll	6	36	Washington State U	4	
Northwestern U	6		Washington U (MO)	4	
Simon Fraser U (CAN)	6		Wesleyan U	4	
U of WI, Oshkosh	6		Western Michigan U	4	
Virginia Comm U	6		Baylor U	3	86
Colby College	6		Boston U	3	
Middlebury College	6		Bowling Green State U	3	
Carnegie Mellon U	5	43	Bucknell U	3	
Michigan State U	5		Colgate U	3	
North TX State U	5		Davidson College	3	
Ohio U	5		Elon U	3	
			Empire State College	3	
			Florida State U	3	
			Furman U	3	
			Hebrew U (Israel)	3	
			Lafayette College	3	
			London U	3	
			Macquarie U (AUS)	3	
			Marshall U	3	

Table 2

Ranking of Institutions Based on Research Productivity (Adjusted Pages) in the *Journal of Economic Education*

School	Total Adj. Pages	Rank 1969-2004	School	Total Adj. Pages	Rank 1969-1979
U of Nebraska, Lincoln	262.8	1	U of MN, Twin Cities	76.5	1
Purdue U	211.47	2	Northern IL U	57	2
Vanderbilt U	197	3	U of IL Urbana-Champ	42.67	3
U of IL, Urbana-Champ	181.17	4	Duke U	41	4
Indiana U, Bloomington	178	5	Vanderbilt U	37	5
IL State U	176.5	6	U of Nebraska, Lincoln	35.67	6
Denison U	136.67	7	Indiana U, Bloomington	30.5	7
U of WI, Madison	121.83	8	U of Georgia	28	8
Stanford U	119.83	9	Furman U	26	9
Mississippi State U	104.17	10	Stanford U	24.5	10
Princeton U	103.07	11	Harvard U	23	11
U of MN, Twin Cities	92.5	12	Purdue U	21	12
Duke U	89.67	13	James Madison U	20	13
U of Georgia	82.33	14	Ohio U	20	
U of Delaware	80.67	15	Clemson U	19.33	15
Northern IL U	79	16	U of WI, Milwaukee	18.5	16
James Madison U	75.08	17	IL State U	18	17
Miami U (OH)	70.67	18	U of CA, Berkeley	18	
U of NC, Chapel Hill	68.67	19	U of North Dakota	17	19
CA State U, Hayward	66	20	U of WI, Madison	16	20
Northwestern U	63.5	21	U of MO, Columbia	15.5	21
Wellesley College	63	22	U of Michigan	13.33	22
Weber State U	62.5	23	Cypress College	13	23
Colby College	55.67	24	Riverside City College	13	
Bradley U	55.5	25	Rice U	13	
U of Melbourne	54	26	CUNY	12	26
Mary Washington College	52.5	27	U of MO, St. Louis	12	
Murray State U	51	28	VPI & State U	11	28
Simon Fraser U (CAN)	50.5	29	Carnegie Mellon U	10.83	29
U of WI, Lacrosse	50.5		Kalamazoo College	10	
			Manhattan College	10	

School	Total Adj. Pages	Rank 1980-1989	School	Total Adj. Pages	Rank 1990-2004
U of IL, Urbana-Champ	98	1	U of Nebraska, Lincoln	136	1
U of Nebraska, Lincoln	91.13	2	Vanderbilt U	114.5	2
Purdue U	85.97	3	Denison U	111.67	3

Indiana U, Bloomington	62.5	4	Purdue U	104.5	4
IL State U	54.5	5	IL State U	104	5
Vanderbilt U	45.5	6	Mississippi State U	87.67	6
U of WI, Madison	43.17	7	Indiana U, Bloomington	85	7
John Carroll U	41.1	8	U of IL, Urbana-Champ	70.5	8
Princeton U	39.67	9	Stanford U	67.33	9
Western IL U	36	10	Miami U (OH)	62.67	10
Washington U (MO)	33	11	U of WI, Madison	62.67	
U of CO, Boulder	32.33	12	Colby College	55.67	12
Duke U	32	13	Princeton U	55.4	13
U of Wyoming	32		U of Melbourne	54	14
Carnegie Mellon U	30.83	15	Murray State U	51	15
London U	30	16	U of NC, Chapel Hill	50.67	16
U of Notre Dame	30		Hamilton College	49.67	17
VA Comm U	28.92	18	Middlebury College	49	18
Bradley U	28.5	19	Northwestern U	46	19
Louisiana State U	28	20	James Madison U	44.83	20
Stanford U	28		U of Delaware	44.5	21
U of Texas, Austin	28		Auburn U	41.67	22
UCLA	27.5	23	U of Richmond	41.5	
U of Delaware	26.5	24	U of WI, Lacrosse	41.5	
U of NV, Las Vegas	26.5		U of WI, Oshkosh	41.5	25
U of MD, College Park	26	26	Wellesley College	41	26
Denison U	25	27	Macquerie U (AUS)	40	27
North TX State U	25		U of MO, Columbia	39.33	28
U of Georgia	25		Lafayette College	39	29
U of South Florida	25		Mary Washington College	38.5	30

The remaining columns in Table 2 denote rankings by separating the entire sample period into shorter periods of time, such as 1969-1979, 1980-1989, and 1990-2004. Some departments consistently produced substantial amounts of scholarship in economic education across all three sample periods (e.g., University of Nebraska at Lincoln, Vanderbilt University, and Purdue University). However, other departments had less research output after 1979. To illustrate a clearer trend in departmental rankings across the different sample periods, we calculated the rank correlation for the Top 15 schools. This information is presented in Table 3. We find that the rank correlation between 1969-1979 and 1980-1989 (1990-2004) is only 0.52 (0.27). This implies that the schools that were research active in economic education in the 1970s put relatively less effort into that area of research in the 1980s. However, the rank correlation between 1980-1989 and 1990-2004 is much larger (0.78), indicating that colleges and universities that were active in economic education in 1980s maintained a similar level of activity into the 1990s and beyond.

Figure 1: Cumulative Distribution of Adjusted Pages Published in the *JEE*

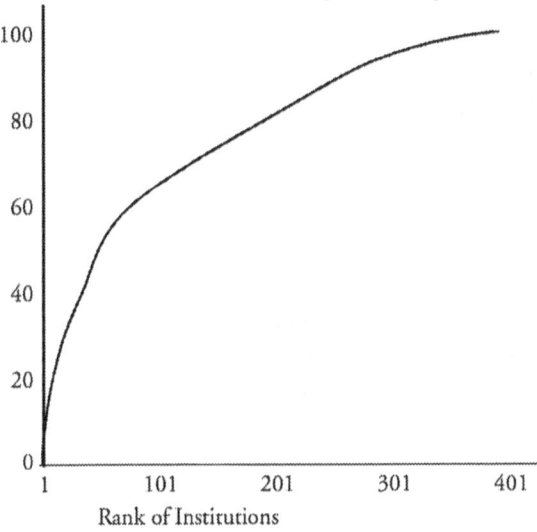

Rank of Institutions

Table 3
Rank Correlations Between Time Periods

Top Schools, 1969-1979	1980-1989 Rank	1990-2004 Rank	Top Schools, 1980-1989	1990-2004 Rank
1. U of MN, Twin Cities	53		1. U of I, Urbana-Champ	8
2. Northern IL U	34		2. U of Nebraska, Lincoln	1
3. U of IL, Urbana-Champ	1	8	3. Purdue U	4
4. Duke U	13	107	4. Indiana U, Bloomington	7
5. Vanderbilt U	6	2	5. IL State U	5
6. U of Nebraska, Lincoln	2	1	6. Vanderbilt U	2
7. Indiana U, Bloomington	4	7	7. U of WI, Madison	10
8. U of Georgia	27	34	8. John Carroll U	
9. Furman U		88	9. Princeton U	13
10. Stanford U	20	9	10. Western IL U	170
11. Harvard U	134	48	11. Washington U (MO)	170
12. Purdue U	3	5	12. U of CO, Boulder	146
13. James Madison U	86	19	13. Duke U	108
Ohio U	95		U of Wyoming	
15. Clemson U	104	266	15. Carnegie Mellon U	109

Rank Correlation (Top 15)
between 1969-1979 and 1980-1989: **0.52**

Rank Correlation (Top 15)   Rank Correlation (Top 15)
between 1969-1979 and 1990-2004: **0.27**   between 1980-1989 and 1990-2004: **0.78**

4. Conclusion

There has been some research on ranking of economics departments worldwide, with past efforts frequently measuring the productivity of departments based on the quantity and/or quality of mainstream research. However, very little research examines the performance of departments according to the quality of education-related research productivity. Using research productivity in economic education as a proxy for teaching quality across institutions, we present a new worldwide ranking system. Because schools with higher rankings usually devote more resources toward improving the quality of instruction in economics, this ranking could help reduce information costs facing consumers (i.e., prospective economics majors) in higher education markets. Moreover, our ranking also shows that some well-established departments may not offer the highest quality experience with regard to economics instruction.

Notes

1. The organizations we excluded from our data set are: Academia Sinica (Taiwan), Advanced Global Energy Solutions, American Federation of Teachers, AmosWEB LLC, Brookings Institution, Bureau of Labor Statistics, *Business Week*, Charles River Associates, Current Economic Analysis Division of Statistics (Ottawa, Canada), Des Moines Independent Community Schools, Dreyfus Corporation, Economic and Social Policy Unit (Canada), Economic Research Services, Inc., Educational Testing Service, Esmee Fairbairn Research Center, Exxon Education Foundation, FDO Partners, LLC, Federal Projects Evaluation, Ford Foundation, Homewood-Flossmoor High School (IL), Joint Council on Economic Education, *Journal of Economic Literature*, Kauffman Foundation, Kemper Financial Services, McGraw-Hill Companies, Ministry of State for Urban Affairs (Ottawa, Canada), National Council on Economic Education, New Jersey Council on Economic Edcuation, Office for Economic Education, Office for Oregon Health Plan Policy and Research, Public Opinion Research Firm of Yankelovich, Skelly and White, Raftelis Environmental Consulting Group, Richfield Senior High School (MN), Schools for Pinellas County (FL) United Energy Resources, Inc., U.S. Consumer Product Safety Commission, U.S. Department of Agriculture, W.E. Upjohn Institute for Employment Research, WhiteNova, World Bank, and International Finance Corporation.

2. The complete ranking can be obtained upon request.

3. We classify three types of universities according to *America's Best Colleges and Universities 2005* at usnews.com, (1) National Universities that offer a wide range of undergraduate majors as well as Master's and Doctoral degrees; (2) Master's degree granting institutions that provide a full range of undergraduate and Master's programs; (3) Liberal Arts colleges that emphasize undergraduate education and award at least half of their degrees in the liberal arts (see usnews.com/usnews/edu/college/rankings/rankindex_brief.php).

References

Dusansky, R. and C.J. Vernon (1998) "Rankings of U.S. economics departments," *Journal of Economic Perspectives* 12: 157-170.

Laband, D.N. (1986) "A ranking of the top U.S. economics departments by research productivity of graduates," *Journal of Economic Education* 17: 70-76.

Lalaitzidakis, P., T.P. Mamuneas and T. Stengos (2003) "Rankings of academic journals and institutions in economics," *Journal of the European Economic Association* 6: 1,346-1,366.

978-0-595-33806-1
0-595-33806-2

www.ingramcontent.com/pod-product-compliance
Lightning Source LLC
Chambersburg PA
CBHW030753180526
45163CB00003B/1005